THE HABSBURG EMPIRE
1804-1918

P9-ECY-984

2.05

HANS KOHN

Professor of History
The City College of New York

AN ANVIL ORIGINAL

under the general editorship of

LOUIS L. SNYDER

D. VAN NOSTRAND COMPANY, INC.

PRINCETON, NEW JERSEY

TORONTO   LONDON

NEW YORK

To the memory of my friend
Dr. Hanns Floch
born in Vienna 23 October 1888
died in San Francisco 22 May 1959

D. VAN NOSTRAND COMPANY, INC.
120 Alexander St., Princeton, New Jersey (*Principal office*); 24 West 40 St., New York, N.Y.
D. VAN NOSTRAND COMPANY (Canada), LTD.
25 Hollinger Rd., Toronto 16, Canada
D. VAN NOSTRAND COMPANY, LTD.
358, Kensington High Street, London, W.14, England

PREFACE

In the nineteenth century the Habsburg Empire continued as the only remnant of the dynastic age. The Habsburgs represented the oldest ruling dynasty in Europe. Originally the Austrian territory which became the center of the Habsburg Empire was called *Ostmark,* Eastern March, a frontier territory of Charlemagne's empire, organized to defend central Europe against the invasions of Asian nomadic tribes. The last of these tribes was the Magyars, who were stopped in their westward drive in the tenth century and thereupon settled in the fertile plains of Hungary along the middle Danube. Austria guarded the road into Europe along the upper Danube, and its capital city, Vienna, was strategically situated where the north–south and east–west axes met in the heart of central Europe.

In the thirteenth century the Habsburgs became the rulers of Austria. From then on they expanded the land under their dominion until it formed an association of various historical-political entities held together by the dynastic tie. Under the impact of the rationalism of the eighteenth century the Habsburgs tried to organize this loose association into a better coordinated administrative whole. The events of the Napoleonic wars forced the Habsburgs to a further step of consolidation, the creation of the Austrian Empire in 1804. But the French Revolution unleashed two modern forces, nationalism and liberalism, which threatened the preservation of the Habsburg Empire, with its roots deep in the premodern age.

In the nineteenth century, the age of nationalism, the complex and multinational empire faced the problem of establishing an order which could give its various nationalities freedom of development and a feeling of equality. Among these nationalities the German element predominated historically as it did in Switzerland. Switzerland

3

succeeded in establishing a stable and democratic order in a multiethnic and multilingual state on the basis of democracy and federalism. In Austria, however, the conservatism of the dynasty and the nationalist intransigence of Magyars and Germans prevented such a development. Under the stresses of the rising forces of nationalism and democracy the Habsburg Empire dissolved in 1918. The First World War, which marked the end of a centuries-old European order, marked also the end of the centuries-old monarchy. It bequeathed to the twentieth century the problem of a federation of equal peoples, not in submission and uniformity, but in freedom and tolerance. The Habsburg Empire had been unable to solve the problem. It has passed into history. But its struggles and efforts in the period from the French Revolution to the First World War illuminate some of the fundamental problems which in an age of worldwide nationalist aspirations face Europe and mankind in the second half of the twentieth century.

HANS KOHN

TABLE OF CONTENTS

5

PART II—SELECTED READINGS

Part I—THE HABSBURG EMPIRE, 1804-1918

GENEALOGICAL TABLES

I. TU FELIX AUSTRIA NUBE

The Habsburgs acquired many crowns and lands not by war but by a dynastic matrimonial policy. Hence the Latin verse "Bella gerant alii, tu, Felix Austria, nube" (Let others fight wars; thou, fortunate Austria, marry), a verse ascribed to the Hungarian King Matthias Corvinus (†1490) in imitation of a line by Ovid.

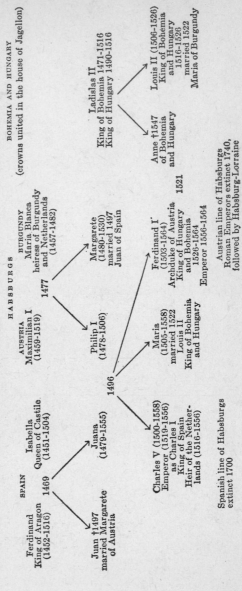

SPAIN

Ferdinand
King of Aragon
(1452-1516)

Isabella
Queen of Castile
(1451-1504)

1469

Juana
(1479-1555)

Juan †1497
married Margarete
of Austria

AUSTRIA

Maximilian I
(1459-1519)

BURGUNDY

Maria Bianca
heiress of Burgundy
and Netherlands
(1457-1482)

1477

HABSBURGS

Philip I
(1478-1506)

Margarete
(1480-1530)
married 1497
Juan of Spain

1496

Charles V (1500-1558)
Emperor (1519-1556)
as Charles I
King of Spain
Heir of the Nether-
lands (1516-1556)

Maria
(1505-1558)
married 1522
Louis II
King of Bohemia
and Hungary

Ferdinand I
(1503-1564)
Archduke of Austria
King of Hungary
and Bohemia
1526-1564
Emperor 1556-1564

BOHEMIA AND HUNGARY

(crowns united in the house of Jagellon)

Ladislas II
King of Bohemia 1471-1516
King of Hungary 1490-1516

Anne †1547
of Bohemia
and Hungary

1521

Louis II (1506-1526)
King of Bohemia
and Hungary
1516-1526
married 1522
Maria of Burgundy

Spanish line of Habsburgs
extinct 1700

Austrian line of Habsburgs
Roman Emperors extinct 1740,
followed by Habsburg-Lorraine

II. THE HOUSE OF HABSBURG-LORRAINE

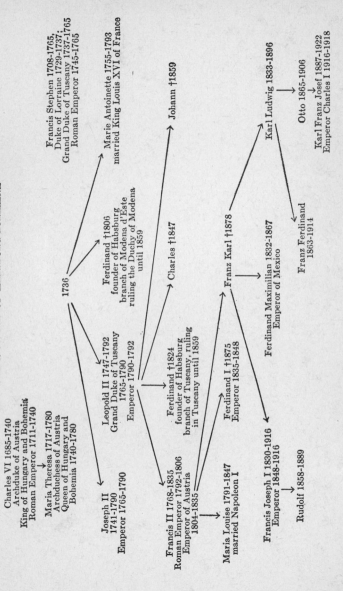

— 1 —

AT THE THRESHOLD OF
A NEW AGE

The House of Habsburg. In 1273 Rudolph of Habsburg (1218-1291) was elected, after a long interregnum, Holy Roman Emperor. His family had important possessions in southwest Germany, in Swabia, and in Switzerland. In 1282 he invested his sons with the duchies of Austria and Styria. The Habsburgs abandoned the Italy-centered imperial ambitions of the Hohenstaufen, the house which had preceded them in the imperial dignity. They were concerned above all with increasing the power of their family or house, the *Hausmacht*. Through acquisition and dynastic marriages they steadily expanded the territory under their rule. In the fourteenth century they acquired peacefully Carinthia, Carniola, Tyrol, Istria, and Trieste. They became thus one of the most powerful princely German families. Duke Rudolph IV (ruled 1358-1365) introduced for his family the new title of Archduke. Through the *privilegium maius*, a forged document, he tried to establish the independence of his lands from Germany. In 1365 he founded the University of Vienna and began to build St. Stephen's Cathedral there. He continued the policy of intermarriage with the ruling houses of the neighboring kingdoms of Bohemia and of Hungary, a policy started by his ancestor Rudolph of Habsburg.

The following century brought the crown of the Holy Roman Empire to the House of Habsburg. It remained in its possession from 1438 to the end of the Empire in 1806 except for the brief period from 1740 to 1745. Empire and Habsburg became almost synonymous. Archduke Frederick V (1415-1493) became Emperor in 1440. He was a man of little energy, who seemed "asleep on his throne." Yet through the marriage of his son Maximilian with the heiress of Burgundy and the Netherlands, whose son in turn married the heiress of Spain and the New World, he laid the foundations of a world empire. He used to inscribe on his buildings and belongings the five vowels A E I O U, which he interpreted as meaning *Austriae est imperare orbi universo* or *Alles Erdreich ist Österreich untertan* (All the earth is subject to Austria). Later this cryptic saying was reinterpreted to mean *Austria erit in orbe ultima* (Austria will be the last on earth).

Maximilian's two grandsons Charles V, who was Holy Roman Emperor from 1519 to 1556, and his brother Ferdinand I, who followed him from 1556 to 1564, faced a twofold task which occupied the Habsburgs for the two following centuries, the defense of Central Europe against the Turks and the defense of the Catholic Church against the Protestant Reformation. Charles V and his descendants ruled in Spain and over the Spanish possessions in Italy, the Low Countries, and the New World. Ferdinand and his descendants ruled in Austria. From the connection with Spain the spirit of the militant Counter Reformation, the art of the Baroque, and the Spanish court ceremonial were taken over by the Austrian Habsburgs. More important was the union of Austria, Bohemia, and Hungary, achieved in 1526 as the result of the famous Viennese double marriage of Maximilian's grandchildren ten years before. In 1526 when King Louis II of Bohemia and Hungary died without issue in the battle of Mohács against the Turks, the Habsburgs inherited the two crowns. As a result of their victory at Mohács the Turks occupied the greater part of Hungary and in 1529 laid siege to Vienna. In the seventeenth century the Habsburgs faced the allied powers of France under Louis XIV and of Turkey; in this contest the year 1683, in which the Turks again besieged Vienna, marked a turning point. From then on the Habsburg armies under Prince Eugene of Savoy (1663-1736) succeeded in reconquering Hungary and driving the Turks back into

the Balkans. The extinction of the Spanish line of the
Habsburgs in 1700 led to a long war of succession, as
the result of which the Austrian Habsburgs acquired the
Spanish Netherlands (Belgium) and the Spanish possessions in Italy.

The House of Habsburg-Lorraine. The male line
of the Austrian Habsburgs became extinct with Charles
VI in 1740. Through the Pragmatic Sanction (1713) and
through negotiations with the Estates of the various lands
under his rule and with the leading foreign powers
Charles secured for the first time the recognition of the
principle of the indivisibility of the Habsburg lands.
What had been previously a purely personal union became now in certain respects for the first time a real
union of countries with independent constitutions and
traditions. At the same time the Pragmatic Sanction stipulated the right of succession, should Charles die without male issue, of his daughter Maria Theresa (1717-
1780). Maria Theresa married in 1736 Francis of Lorraine (1708-1765). In 1737, after the extinction of the
House of Medici, Francis became Grand Duke of Tuscany in exchange for his native Lorraine; Maria Theresa
followed her father in 1740 as Archduchess of Austria
and Queen of Bohemia and Hungary. Her husband
Francis became in 1745 Holy Roman Emperor. Their
descendants, the House of Habsburg-Lorraine, preserved
on the whole the Habsburg traits. Of their three oldest
sons Joseph II followed his father in 1765 as Holy Roman
Emperor and inherited from his mother in 1780 the rule
of Austria, Bohemia, and Hungary; Leopold became
Grand Duke of Tuscany, and Ferdinand Duke of Modena.

In the eighteenth century the Habsburgs faced new
problems, fundamentally different from those of the seventeenth century. The Turkish menace was replaced by
that of Russia; Spain, now under a younger branch of
the House of Bourbon, was allied with France; in Germany the rapid rise of the House of Hohenzollern in
Prussia contested the leading position of the Habsburgs
in the Holy Roman Empire and prevented its consolidation; finally, the French Revolution unleashed new pop-

ular forces which threatened the very foundation of traditional Habsburg rule.

Maria Theresa and, above all, her son Joseph tried to reform and to rationalize the administration of their so widely diversified lands. A typical enlightened despot, Joseph II wished to create a progressive centralized state but proceeded without regard to the ancient traditions which were deeply rooted in the people's minds. When he died in 1790 his brother Leopold succeeded him as Emperor and as ruler of the Austrian lands. He was much more cautious than Joseph, but he, too, was touched by the spirit of the Enlightenment. On June 4, 1789, he wrote to his sister that it seemed to him "that one is happiest when a country has a constitution. . . . The nation is attached to it, and . . . it is much easier to direct it towards its own well-being and happiness, which is the only end for which every government is instituted."

Leopold welcomed the beginning of the French Revolution from which he expected a regeneration of France, which would become a model which all sovereigns in Europe would have to follow, willingly or unwillingly. "The only purpose of societies and governments," he wrote in another letter to his sister on January 25, 1790, "is the welfare of the individuals. . . . A sovereign who does not abide by [the fundamental law of the country] thereby forfeits his position . . . and henceforth no one is obliged to obey him; the executive power is vested in the sovereign, but the legislative in the people and its representatives." Unfortunately, these principles did not prevail. In 1792 Leopold died and was followed by his son Francis II, who ruled from 1792 to 1806 as the last Holy Roman Emperor. He was a man of narrow mind, strictly conservative and without any imagination. In the year when he ascended to the throne, the French Revolution, with the overthrow of the monarchy, took a new and frightening turn which disillusioned many of its early adherents. The same year also saw the start of the long wars between revolutionary France, soon to be consolidated and led to new triumphs under Napoleon, and old Europe. In this old Europe and its defense Austria under the Habsburgs played a leading role.

The Wars Against the Revolution.   The war which started as a war of coalition in 1792 ended in 1797 with the peace of Campoformio, in which the Habsburgs lost Belgium and Lombardy and gained Venetia and Dalmatia. During the war Prussia abandoned the coalition in 1795 and made its peace with revolutionary France. A second war against France (1799-1801) ended again with a French victory and began the period of the final agony of the Holy Roman Empire, which was forced to cede the left bank of the Rhine to France. In May 1804 Napoleon assumed the title of Emperor of the French. To counter this move Francis proclaimed himself in August 1804 Emperor of Austria, an entirely new title, which for the first time established a unified denomination for all the various kingdoms and lands under Habsburg rule, which however retained their ancient titles, constitutions, and privileges. The Habsburgs had been for centuries elected Holy Roman Emperors; now they became hereditary Austrian Emperors. A new attempt to stop the French drive towards further expansion, undertaken jointly by Austria and Russia in 1805, ended in failure when the French won the battle of Austerlitz on December 5. As a result Napoleon organized the German princes in a Confederation of the Rhine which in close union with France was to replace the Holy Roman Empire. Faced by this situation Francis II dissolved the Holy Roman Empire in August 1806. He was from that time on Francis I, Emperor of Austria. The new Empire adopted as its own the black and yellow colors of the old empire and the two-headed eagle in its coat of arms.

In the long war against Europe the victories of the French armies were due not only to Napoleon's superior generalship but to the aroused patriotic spirit of the French people. No such modern patriotism or feeling of nationhood existed in Austria. Instead the *ancien régime* attachment to provincial traditions prevailed. Francis was unable to understand the needs of the new age. He was the embodiment of mechanized bureaucracy, and deeply distrusted the people and any spontaneous forces. When someone was recommended to him for being an ardent patriot, the Emperor gave the characteristic reply: "He may be a patriot for Austria but the question is whether he is a patriot for me." The inefficiency and obsoleteness of the administration became fully manifest in the wars against the revolution. The Emperor's younger brothers, Archdukes Karl (1771-1847) and Johann (1782-1859), both much more popular than he was but for that reason distrusted by him, repeatedly demanded reforms and tried to activize the administration and the people. Only in the year 1809, when Austria alone took up arms against Napoleon, the government made a short-lived effort to arouse a national consciousness among the people. A periodical was founded "to bring the inhabitants of the hereditary lands of the Emperor and King more closely together, to make them mutually better acquainted, and to promote love of the fatherland through its knowledge."

But the war was lost; though Archduke Karl won a victory at Aspern in May, he was defeated at Wagram in July. The peace which followed imposed heavy sacrifices on Austria, which lost its southwestern provinces, including Istria and Dalmatia, to France. These provinces were organized by the new ruler into a unit called Illyria. Exhausted, Austria made her peace with France and Francis' daughter Marie Louise married Napoleon. Their marriage was arranged by Count (later Prince) Klemens Metternich (1773-1859), the descendant of an aristocratic Rhineland family who had entered Austria's diplomatic services. In 1795 he took the granddaughter of Count Wenzel Anton Kaunitz (1711-1794) as his first wife. Kaunitz had been Austrian foreign minister for thirty-nine years, from 1753 to 1792. In 1809 Metternich followed him as foreign minister and for thirty-nine years he was the leading personality in Austrian life. His name was used as a symbol for the whole age which lasted from the defeat of the French Revolution in 1814 to the outbreak of the new French revolution of 1848. In 1829 Metternich, while remaining foreign minister, was named Chancellor.

After Napoleon's defeat in Russia and his retreat to German soil, Austria under Metternich's leadership joined Russia and Prussia in August 1813 in the war against Napoleon. After Napoleon's final defeat on French soil the congress of the victors met in Vienna in October 1814 to settle the conditions of peace, a task achieved on June 9, 1815. During the conference, at which Metternich was the dominant figure, disputes among the allies broke out about the future of Poland, through the incorporation of which Russia wished to move her frontiers far to the west, and of Saxony, a German buffer state between Austria and Prussia. In these disputes Prussia sided with Russia, whereas the Austrian position was backed by Britain and France.

The Austrian Empire. In spite of the longings of some German patriots, the Holy Roman Empire was not resurrected in 1815. Francis I, whose mind was entirely devoid of romantic imagination, not only rejected this restoration, he renounced also all Habsburg possessions which were separated territorially from the main body of his domains. These possessions included Belgium and the various Swabian lands in southwest Germany which had belonged to the Habsburgs for many centuries; among them the most important was the Breisgau on the upper Rhine, with Freiburg as its capital. For this loss Austria was compensated by the acquisition of Lombardy and Venetia in northern Italy. The Habsburg lands formed now for the first time a contiguous territorial unit. The Illyrian provinces were restored to Austria, as was Tyrol, which during the wars had been ceded to Bavaria; from Bavaria Austria also received the former archbishopric of Salzburg. From a geographic point of view the new Austrian Empire formed predominantly the basin of the middle Danube. But some of its most important parts—Bohemia and Galicia in the north and Illyria in the south—did not belong to the Danubian system. The Danube flowed into the Black Sea, whereas the waters of Bohemia emptied into the North Sea, those of Galicia into the Baltic Sea, and those of Illyria into the Adriatic.

During the Napoleonic Wars the new ideas and aspirations of nationalism began to stir small circles of intellectuals and writers among the Germans and Italians.

They now raised demands for a closer political unity of all the various peoples speaking the German or the Italian language. The Congress of Vienna did not heed these demands. The Holy Roman Empire had been a supranational successor to the ancient Roman Empire. It was not a German nation-state. The creation of such a nation-state seemed premature in 1815, but there was general agreement that some form of cooperation among all German princes was needed. Accordingly, thirty-nine sovereign German-speaking states were united in a German Confederation, in which the two strongest powers were Austria and Prussia. Neither of them was a purely German state and only a part of the Austrian and Prussian territories entered into the German Confederation. The latter was a loose association, formed primarily for the purpose of common defense and for maintaining peace in Germany. A permanent Diet of governmental representatives met in Frankfort on the Main, and Austria was by statute its presiding power. Thus even after the end of the Holy Roman Empire the Habsburgs preserved the primacy among the German princes which they had enjoyed for the preceding four centuries. In addition they occupied a leading role in Italy.

In Italy no confederacy after the German model was created, for Italy had never been united since Roman times. The predominance of Habsburg influence there was based upon the fact that Lombardy and Venetia now formed part of Austria and that junior branches of the Habsburgs ruled in Tuscany and Modena. Thus in outward appearance the Austrian Empire emerged greatly strengthened from the long wars against the revolution. Vienna was for a short time the diplomatic capital of Europe. In population, Austria ranked second only to Russia among the great powers. But this apparent strength had no sufficiently firm foundation in the people. This seemed to matter little in 1815, when absolutism was firmly restored all over central and southern Europe. Yet this very same absolutism prevented a flexible accommodation to the new forces of constitutional liberalism and nationalism, which soon began to reassert themselves.

To prevent their spread, the Emperors of Russia and Austria and the King of Prussia signed in Vienna on September 26, 1815, the Holy Alliance, an alliance of three Christian monarchs, each representing one of the three great branches of Christianity. The document in which they promised to keep international peace and to govern their peoples according to "the sublime truths taught by the eternal religion of God, our Saviour," was no more than an expression of pious wishes, but it was regarded in the years to follow as an affirmation of the determination of the three Eastern Monarchs to maintain and promote absolutism in their own lands and abroad, and to prevent or suppress any movements for the reform of government and the establishment of liberties and rights of their citizens, movements they regarded as stimulated by an international revolutionary conspiracy.

The Peoples of the Habsburg Monarchy. The Habsburg Empire inherited a supranational character from the Holy Roman Empire. The Habsburgs insisted on introducing German as the one language of administration throughout their lands, but this effort was made for the purely practical reason that it let their possessions be more unified and more rationally administered, and not out of any German nationalism. The Habsburg rulers themselves represented the mentality of the prenationalist age and by the end of the Napoleonic Wars hardly any conscious nationalism had yet arisen among the various peoples under Habsburg rule. The court aristocracy largely wrote and spoke in French; the educated and commercial classes in all the provinces spoke and wrote in German; the official language in Hungary was Latin; only the peasants used the various vernaculars, which in many cases had not yet developed into full-fledged literary languages. The process of national awakening among the various nationalities started only in the decades following the downfall of Napoleon. It took a different course among the various peoples according to their historical status and their social structure.

History divided the peoples of the Austrian Monarchy into those, like the Magyars, the Czechs, and the Poles, who could look back to, and glory in, a past in which they had formed important states of their own; and others, like the Slovaks, Slovenes, and Rumanians, who had no historical "rights" to revive and to defend but could base their demands on the "natural" right of national self-determination. Some of the former demanded the restoration of their historical entities in their historical borders. The two most imporant of these "historical" realms were the lands of the Crown of St. Stephen (the kingdom of Hungary) and the lands of the Crown of St. Wenceslaus (the kingdom of Bohemia). But the historical territories nowhere coincided with the ethnic borders of the present time. The claims of the nonhistorical nationalities therefore conflicted with those of the "historical" ones, and the difficulties created by these conflicts outlived even the Habsburg Empire and troubled the existence of its succession states after 1918.

Just as important as the difference of historical status was the difference in social structure. Some of the nationalities consisted at the beginning of the nineteenth century only of peasant populations and had therefore no social influence or economic power; others, like the Magyars, Poles, Germans, and Italians, could count on a numerous and wealthy landowning aristocracy and a prosperous middle class. This disparity of social structure embittered in many cases the struggle among the nationalities. The social mobility and the freedom of movement acquired in the nineteenth century complicated this struggle by the influx of the peasant masses of the less developed peoples into the cities, the national character of which underwent thereby a change. In many cases the growth of national consciousness and the desire for social emancipation went together. The industrial revolution and urbanization of the century accelerated this process.

Among the various nationalities of the Austrian Empire none formed a majority. Even the Germans and the Magyars each represented less than a fourth of the population. The Germans lived in a compact mass in the old hereditary lands of the Habsburgs, in Danubian Austria and in the northeastern Alps. The Magyars lived east of them, in the plain between the Danube and the

Tisza rivers. South of the Germans and Magyars lived the southern Slavs or Yugoslavs (the word *yug* meaning "south"). The southern Slavs were divided into three different peoples—Slovenes to the west, Serbs to the east, and the Croats in between. The Slovenes and Croats intermingled with Italians who lived in the more important cities along the Adriatic coast and, of course, in Lombardy and Venetia. North of the Germans and Magyars lived other Slav peoples—the Czechs in the west, the Slovaks in the center, and the Ruthenians or Carpatho-Ukrainians in the east. North of the Carpathian Mountains, in the province of Galicia, there lived Poles and Ukrainians, both Slavic peoples. In the neighboring province of Bucovina Rumanians, Ukrainians, and Germans intermingled. East of Hungary was the province of Transylvania, where Rumanian, Magyar, and German settlers lived. German settlers could be found as minority groups throughout the Empire; the largest and most compact of these groups was in the northwest, in Bohemia and Moravia alongside the Czech population, above all on the slopes of the Sudeten mountains.

Some of these nationalities—the Czechs, Slovaks, Slovenes, Croats, and Magyars—were to be found only in the Habsburg Empire. Others lived contiguous to larger groups speaking the same language outside the Habsburg Empire. These were the Germans, the Italians, the Poles, the Ukrainians, the Rumanians, and the Serbs. In the nineteenth century, the age of nationalism, the populations regarding themselves as belonging to the same ethnic and linguistic group felt more and more the desire for establishing a bond of unity across historical or political borders, and this trend created powerful centrifugal forces threatening to disintegrate the Habsburg Empire.

This great variety of ethnic origins, languages, and historical memories in its population made the Austrian Empire the most pronounced multinational state in nineteenth-century Europe. The chief tie which helped preserve unity was loyalty to the dynasty, a loyalty felt most strongly in the army and in the higher bureaucracy. Another tie strengthening unity was the predominance of the Catholic Church. Protestants, Greek Orthodox,

Jews, and Mohammedans numbered about 20 per cent of the population—Mohammedans were only represented in Bosnia-Herzegovina which in 1878 came under Austro-Hungarian administration; Jews were most numerous in Bucovina and Galicia, Protestants in Hungary, the Greek Orthodox among the Serbs and the Ukrainians. In the course of the nineteenth century, with religion losing its dominant grip on the mind and with nationalism rising, the Catholic Church no longer presented as strong a cementing link as it did in preceding centuries. The Catholic Italians faced the Catholic Croats in as bitter a national struggle as did the Catholic Germans the Catholic Slovenes or the Catholic Magyars the Catholic Slovaks.

Thus towards the end of the nineteenth century, loyalty to the dynasty remained as the sole centripetal emotional force in the multinational empire. As the result of the growth of the middle class in the nineteenth century—a growth which coincided with the rise of nationalism—the armed forces and the bureaucracy took on a stronger middle-class character in their composition and thus lost more and more of their originally supra-national dynastic loyalty. Yet this loyalty continued among large parts of the population even into the twentieth century. Only the First World War, which destroyed the magic of dynastic loyalty in many other lands, put an end to it in the Habsburg monarchy too.

It is true that other forces favored the maintenance of Austrian imperial unity. This unity represented a source of military and economic strength, from which the security and the peace of the various nationalities and their industrial and commercial growth profited. But such "rational" arguments prevailed little at a time when nationalism emotionally stirred the masses and inclined them more and more to regard national independence and power as a supreme goal to be often achieved at the expense of neighboring fellow nationalities. In their conservatism and their distrust of new ideas and popular movements the Habsburgs made no effort to create an Austrian idea which would stir the peoples and provide the basis for a new loyalty. Nor were they willing to curb to a sufficient degree the domineering instincts of the three most advanced and most aristocratic nationalities—the Magyars, the Germans, and the Poles—so as to allow the development of a cohesive federation based upon the equality of all nationalities. Such an equality was not possible on the basis of the aristocratic structure which survived in Austria into the second half of the nineteenth century and in Hungary even until after 1918. Such an equality could be established only on broad democratic foundations. It demanded the recognition of the rise of the middle classes through education and economic progress and an active promotion of the interests of the peasants and soon of the industrial workers too, throughout the Empire. The opposition to such a program was best expressed by Prince Metternich. (*See Reading No. 1.*) But the spirit of monarchical absolutism survived even his downfall.

THE DEFEAT OF CONSTITUTIONAL LIBERALISM

The Age of Stagnation. The three decades which followed the victory over Napoleon were to a growing degree an era of stagnation. Even Metternich proposed some very modest constitutional reforms, but the Emperor shelved them and Metternich in his hedonistic indolence did not insist but was glad to let things go. Financial mismanagement and the backwardness of the system of taxation brought recurrent threats of state bankruptcy. Economically and culturally Austria fell behind other German states, above all Prussia. Whereas Prussia prepared its leadership in the unification of Germany by initiating a customs union embracing most German states, Austria shut herself off from the rest of Germany by high tariff walls. Equally pernicious was the cultural iron curtain drawn around the country. Teachers and students in the schools, especially in the universities, were closely supervised and the students were forbidden to study abroad. The few independent scholars or thinkers— among them Bernhard Bolzano (1781-1848), professor of philosophy at Prague and a Catholic priest—were dismissed. Emperor Francis declared before secondary-school teachers in Laibach in 1821: "I do not need scholars but obedient citizens. Your task is to educate the youth in this sense. Whosoever serves me, must teach what I command. Those who are unable to do that or wish to bring new ideas can leave or I shall remove them."

The very numerous and poorly paid bureaucracy

worked extremely slowly. Many affairs were dealt with
by not dealing with them. The most efficient branch of
the government was the police department, which was
directed from 1817 to 1848 by Count Joseph Sedlnitzky
(1778-1855), president of the supreme police and of the
censorship office. Things got worse when Francis fell
seriously ill in 1826, after which the signs of his growing
senility increased rapidly. When he died in 1835, he was
followed by his son Ferdinand, a kindly but sickly
imbecile. The principle of legitimacy had to be upheld.
Such a principle has nowhere as dangerous consequences
as in an absolutist monarchy. Had the throne of Austria
become occupied in 1792 or in 1835 by Archduke Karl
or Archduke Johann, the history of Austria might have
taken a different turn. When in 1835 Archduke Karl,
who lived in retirement, hired Joseph Baron Kalchberg
as tutor for his sons, he told him: "Bring them up according to your convictions, and should these sometimes
not coincide with mine I shall know how to resign myself.
My sons will live in another era and they should be
educated for that era. I know very well that I harbor
some prejudices, but they cannot be decisive for the
education of my sons. Only that which will be useful to
them should be considered. Above all, oppose all inclination towards absolutism. It has outlived its day."

To assist the new Emperor, a State Council was appointed under the presidency of the new ruler's uncle,
Archduke Louis, with Prince Metternich and Count
Franz Anton Kolowrat (1778-1861) as members. The
new State Council did not improve matters. Metternich
and Kolowrat hated each other and were not on speaking
terms. Kolowrat, though an arch-conservative too, loved
"to play the liberal opponent of the Metternich system."
Matters went from bad to worse. They were made bear-
able by the fact that the government showed no special
preference in state employment for any one nationality,
that the officials were on the whole men of personal
integrity, and that the well-known Viennese character
traits of *Gemütlichkeit* and *Schlamperei*, though they
enhanced inefficiency, left wide loopholes for the human
—all-too-human. But, as one of the most conservative high

officials, Count Joseph Alexander von Hüber (1811-1892), wrote, "there was [heard] not a single word that spoke to the heart, to the noble instincts, to the higher feelings of the nation. There was nothing but silence and immobility."

In literature only the theater, in which the Viennese people have always taken a profound interest, prospered. The Court Theater, the *Burgtheater,* under the direction of Joseph Schreyvogel (1768-1832) became the foremost stage in Germany. Eduard von Bauernfeld (1802-1890) provided it with comedy, and Franz Grillparzer (1791-1872) was one of the great classical drama writers of German literature. In the suburban theaters popular farce often mixed merriment with profundity. Its two most prominent authors and actors were Ferdinand Raimund (1790-1836) and Johann Nestroy (1801-1862). The famous musical period in Viennese history had come to an end before 1830. Its greatest representative, Ludwig van Beethoven, who was born in 1770, lived in Vienna after 1792 and died there in 1827. The following year Franz Schubert, thirty-one years old, died in the greatest poverty; this incomparable master of the German song (*Lied*) was buried beside Beethoven.

The Awakening of the Peoples. The years of stagnation at the center of the monarchy did not mean a similar stagnation in the life of the various peoples forming the Habsburg Empire. Three influences converged to transform the life of these peoples and to arouse demands in them unknown in the preceding age. The first of these influences was the revival of the ideas of constitutionalism and nationalism, which after Napoleon's defeat in 1814 began to reassert themselves in western and southern Europe in the 1820's and reached their first climax after the French revolution in July 1830. Slowly these ideas penetrated into central Europe. The policy of strict seclusion and censorship could not stop them. The second of these influences originated in the educational policies of the Habsburg monarchs in the period of the Enlightenment. These policies resulted in the growing literacy of the peasantry and its need for developing the vernacular languages. The third, and

perhaps most important, influence, above all among the
less developed nationalities, was that of German Romanti-
cism with its emphasis on folk traditions and folk song.
The German writer Johann Gottfried Herder (1744-
1803) had put forward the theory that the people's most
precious possession was its mother tongue as spoken by
the common folk, and that man's mind could be truly
developed only in the mother tongue, not in a foreign
or universal language. Herder encouraged the intellectuals
of the smaller nationalities who had been educated in
Latin, French, or German to turn their attention to the
cult of the mother tongue, and that meant to the language
spoken by the peasants.

With the exception of the Magyars, the other peoples
did not at that time raise political demands. Their nationalism started as a cultural awakening, not under the
leadership of politicians or administrators but under that
of publicists, historians, and poets, whose first task was
to create a literary language and to spread national consciousness among the educated classes. The Czechs offered the outstanding example of this cultural awakening
among the Slav peoples. Josef Jungmann (1773-1847)
wrote the first great Czech dictionary and translated many
Western works into Czech. Even more important was the
work of the historian František Palacký (1798-1876)
who in his history of the Czech nation gave a new interpretation of its past, according to which the late
medieval Hussite movement with its reformatory and
"liberal" tendencies laid the foundations of democracy
among the Czechs. Palacký himself was a Protestant,
as was the Slovak poet Jan Kollár (1793-1852), who
in his book of poetry *Slava's Daughter* praised the unity
of all Slavic-speaking peoples, their humanity and their
future greatness. The Czech cultural awakening influenced
also their Slovak neighbors. They too, began to develop
a literary language out of the peasant dialect; but owing
to the oppression which they suffered at the hands of
the Magyars they progressed much more slowly than
the Czechs.

A similar cultural development set in among the
southern Slavs, the Slovenes and the Croats. The Slovenes

were a people without political history; but under Bartholomäus Kopitar (1780-1844), a highly renowned philologist of the period, they developed their own language. His disciple France Prešeren (1800-1847) was the first Slovene poet to revive the folklore of his people. The Slovenes, like the Croats, formed part of Illyria, the French province which Napoleon created. Under his administration the development of the native languages was promoted. But the Croats (unlike the Slovenes) could look back on a political existence of many centuries. After a brief independence in the tenth and eleventh centuries the kingdom of Croatia became an autonomous part of the kingdom of Hungary. Its official name was the "Triune Kingdom of Croatia, Slavonia, and Dalmatia." Croatia had its own Diet, which like the Hungarian Diet used Latin as the official language. The establishment of Illyria by Napoleon stimulated the growth of an "Illyrian" cultural movement which hoped to unite all the southern Slavs. Its leader was Ljudevit Gaj (1809-1871). It stimulated also Croat determination to resist the encroachment of Magyar nationalism on Croatian autonomy rights.

Even more than the Croats, the Magyars were a people with a proud national past, the consciousness of which was kept alive throughout the centuries. The Turkish domination of the larger part of Hungary in the sixteenth and seventeenth centuries prevented there the weakening of the power of the Estates which happened elsewhere in Europe under the impact of centralizing monarchist absolutism. The Hungarian Estates, composed mostly of the Hungarian nobility, showed a spirit of independence and a ruthless will to defend their class and national position not found in other provinces of the Habsburg Empire. The feudalist nationalist spirit of the Hungarian nobility survived unbroken until 1918 and even until 1945. But until the first part of the nineteenth century Hungary was a supranational nobilitarian class society. Under the influence of the nineteenth-century ideas of linguistic nationalism Hungary transformed itself into a Magyar nation-state in which the Magyar feudal ruling class continued to control the state.

In the first part of the nineteenth century, representatives of the gentry and of the rising middle class promoted a cultural development of the Magyar language, demanded its introduction as the official language of administration and legislation instead of Latin, and consciously wished to make the Magyar element the dominant one among all the various nationalities in the formerly supranational kingdom; the new development introduced a regime of oppression for the non-Magyar nationalities, the Slovaks and Serbs, the Ruthenians and the Rumanians. At the same time the rising new classes wished to broaden the national basis of the new nation-state, by introducing a number of social reforms which would modernize the structure of the state. The leader of a moderate reform movement was Count Istvan Széchenyi (1791-1860), whereas the new nationalism was represented above all by Lajos Kossuth (1802-1894), who in his newspaper *Pesti Hirlap,* founded in 1841, attacked the privileges of the aristocrats.

A political historical consciousness similiar to that of the Magyars was alive among the Poles. That part of Poland which as a result of the partitions of the late eighteenth century had fallen under Austrian domination enjoyed in the nineteenth century a much greater political freedom than the parts that had come under Russian or Prussian domination. The influence of the Polish nobility over the peasant masses remained in Austria stronger than in the other parts of former Poland. This Polish nobility kept the Ukrainian peasants who formed the major portion of the population in eastern Galicia in social and also in national submission, refusing to recognize their national rights and even their existence as a separate nationality. In this policy the Polish nobility found the nationalist support of the rising Polish middle class.

The unrest of the Prussian Poles of Poznań in 1844 threatened to spread to the Poles in Austrian Galicia, where the city of Cracow formed a small independent republic, established at the Congress of Vienna. The Polish national uprising in Galicia was thwarted by an uprising of the Polish peasant masses in western Galicia, who in bitter resentment of their social position turned against the nobility. As a result Austria occupied the city republic of Cracow. Dissatisfaction of the Polish and above all the Ukrainian peasant masses provided the Austrian government with a means of pressure on the Polish nobility. As a result the latter showed a greater willingness to cooperate with the Austrian government provided that the social position of the nobility and the privileged national position of the Poles in Galicia was preserved. In the stormy years of 1848-1849 the Poles kept relatively quiet.

Different was the situation among the Italians. With the rise of Italian nationalism in the early nineteenth century, the Italians, who (unlike the Hungarians and the Poles) had never formed an independent political state, could nevertheless identify themselves with the proud Roman tradition; and in its name they demanded the creation of a unified Italian state, a demand which was incompatible with the Austrian possession of Lombardy and Venetia. The Italian demand for the "redemption" of the "unredeemed" Italian lands—*Italia irredenta*—the Italian-speaking parts of the Habsburg Empire, caused the Italians to go to war against Austria four times in the nineteenth century—in 1848, in 1859, in 1866, and in 1915. In 1815 the Austrian government organized Lombardy and Venetia into a "kingdom" of their own, separated administratively from the rest of the Habsburg Empire. This kingdom did not include the Italians living in the older Habsburg lands, in the southernmost part of Tyrol, and in the Austrian Adriatic provinces, above all in the seaports of Trieste and Fiume. The Italians in Austria did not suffer from the bitter social antagonisms under which the Magyars and Poles labored. They had a very highly developed middle class and their nobility enjoyed no exclusive feudal privileges. In Lombardy and Venetia the middle classes and the nobility cooperated in the years before 1848 in their opposition to the Austrian regime. It was in Milan, the capital of Lombardy, that the revolutionary fire of 1848 ignited the first sparks.

1848: Hopes and Defeats. In February 1848 the

monarchy was overthrown in France and the republic proclaimed. The events of the following months throughout central Europe revealed how strong the unrest under the cover of absolutism had been. The year started with greatest hopes. It ended in chaos and disillusionment. Nowhere did events offer as complex a spectacle as in the Habsburg monarchy. But the complexity was not the cause of failure. In Germany and in Italy the problem of political national unification under a regime of constitutional liberty was much less complex, yet in both countries by 1849 the attempts at its solution had failed. In the territories of the Habsburg monarchy the problem was complicated by the fact that there were several nationalities striving for unity and liberty and they all acted at cross purposes. The situation was made even more confused, because the Germans and the Italians in the Habsburg monarchy participated in the general national movements of their fellow nationals who lived outside the Habsburg Empire.

From the beginning the two trends of the revolution were in conflict—the liberal trend, which stressed the introduction of modern constitutions securing the rights and liberty of the individual against authority, and the nationalist trend, which wished to strengthen the authority of the national collectivity, and this in most cases at the expense of other nationalities. In this conflict national aspirations took precedence over human liberty. (*See Reading No. 2.*) The struggle among the various nationalities themselves doomed the revolution and gave the Habsburgs the opportunity of reëstablishing their absolutist rule. But the unfortunate consequences of the nationalists' conflicting ambitions did not remain confined to the year 1848 nor to the Habsburg Empire. They survived its disintegration and plagued central Europe after 1918. They were largely responsible for offering first totalitarian Germany and then totalitarian Russia the opportunity for imposing their control and ideology on the whole of central Europe.

The revolutionary events of 1848 in Austria unfolded in five separate, and yet interconnected developments— among the Germans (Vienna), the Czechs (Prague), the

Magyars (Budapest), the Croatians (Zagreb or Agram), and the Italians (Milan and Venice). At the very beginning stood an event, welcomed by all: the pressure of the students of Vienna forced Metternich's resignation on March 13. (*See Readings No. 3 and 4.*) Two days later the Habsburg court promised the introduction of a constitution. By that time unrest had already seized the Germans and Italians throughout their lands, and the Hungarian Diet, which had been meeting in Pressburg (Bratislava) since November 1847, demanded an extension of Hungary's home rule. The spokesmen of the German national movement met in Heidelberg on March 6 to prepare the convocation of an elected German parliament in Frankfort on the Main. As Bohemia formed a part of the German Confederation, the Czech national leader Palacký was invited to attend. He replied in a memorable letter which for the first time defined the Czech national point of view and assigned to the continuation of the Habsburg monarchy an important European task. Austria was to form a bulwark against the conquest of central eastern Europe by Russian or German expansionism. It was to provide a protective shield over the various central eastern European nationalities giving them at the same time the opportunity for a free national development on the footing of equality. (*See Reading No. 5.*)

The nationality conflicts in the Habsburg monarchy were before 1848 little understood or known in the west, with the exception of the Italian demands for independence. Even before the Paris revolution of 1848, unrest had swept the Italian peninsula. There were bloody riots in Milan and elsewhere, and the rulers of Naples, Piedmont, and Tuscany had been forced or induced to grant constitutions. In the five days from March 18 to 22, 1848, a popular uprising freed Milan from Austrian occupation, and Venice followed suit under the leadership of Daniele Manin (1804-1857). The Piedmontese army came to the help of the insurrectionists, but it was disastrously defeated at Custoza near Verona by the Austrian forces under General Joseph Wenzel Count Radetzky (1766-1858). By August the Austrians were again in control of

Milan. The first round of the revolutionary war in Italy had ended in a resounding military victory for the Habsburgs.

But already two months before their triumph in Italy the military forces had reasserted themselves, on behalf of the Habsburg monarchy, in street fighting against Czech radicals in Prague. There the Austrian army did not face a strong national army as it did in Italy. Its adversaries were mostly students on improvised barricades. Yet the reëstablishment of order by the commanding general Prince Alfred Windischgrätz (1787-1862) on June 12 marked a turning point in the course of the events of 1848. In those days a congress of the Austrian Slavs, under Palacký's chairmanship, was meeting in the Bohemian capital. Its leaders were moderate liberals who wished to preserve and strengthen the Habsburg monarchy though at the same time to reform it. In view of the events of June 12 the Austro-Slav congress could not finish its deliberations and was dispersed. The antagonism not only of the reactionary but also of the radical Germans to the Czech and Slav nationalist aspirations within the Habsburg monarchy was so great that the Viennese democrats jubilantly welcomed Windischgrätz's triumph. (*See Reading No. 6.*) Yet only four months later the same Windischgrätz, who was in the eyes of the liberals and radicals the most hated aristocrat of old Austria, suppressed with his army a popular uprising of the Germans in Vienna, and a number of German democrats perished in the ensuing reign of terror.

Meanwhile the court had proclaimed a constitution and as a result a parliamentary assembly called *Reichstag* met in July in Vienna. Its most important decision, and the one lasting achievement of the Revolution of 1848, was the complete emancipation of the Austrian peasants. On July 24 Hans Kudlich (1823-1917), then a law student at the University of Vienna and the youngest member of the *Reichstag* (he later emigrated to the United States), moved that "from now on all servile relationships, together with all rights and obligations based upon them, are abolished." Though the peasants were the only class to profit from the revolution, they nowhere actively participated in it and remained unshaken in their loyalty to the dynasty.

When the October uprising broke out in Vienna, the court escaped to the quietness of the small Moravian town of Olmütz (Olomouc) and the parliament was transferred to the nearby town of Kremsier (Kroměříž). There it deliberated on the future constitution of Austria, which was adopted on March 7, 1849. The Empire was to be reorganized on the basis of the autonomy of its various parts and of the equality of its various nationalities. "All the national groups of the Empire have equal rights"—so read the draft proposed by Palacký's son-in-law, František Ladislav Rieger (1818-1903). "Each of them has an inviolable right to the preservation and cultivation of its nationality in general and its language in particular. Legal equality of all languages customarily spoken in school, governmental agencies, and public life will be guaranteed by the state." The *Reichstag* was to consist of two chambers, of which (after the model of the United States, which had been accepted the year before in the federal constitution of Switzerland) the lower one represented the people and the upper one the various lands. This Kremsier constitution, which unfortunately never went into force, was the only instance in modern Austrian history in which all the various nationalities through their representatives arrived at an agreed-upon solution of the difficult problem of how to reconcile the unity of the Empire with the rights and freedoms of its component nationalities.

The Kremsier constitution was not accepted by the court because by that time the military victories of Radetzky and Windischgrätz had restored its confidence. In November Windischgrätz's brother-in-law Prince Felix Schwarzenberg (1800-1852) became prime minister. He was a proud aristocrat, dedicated to the restoration of the grandeur of the Habsburg monarchy and of its leading position in Germany and Italy. He gained an easy ascendancy over the young man who at the age of eighteen became Emperor of Austria on December 2, 1848. Because it was generally recognized that the Emperor Ferdinand's mind was too feeble to hold the Empire together, he abdicated in favor of his nephew Franz (1830-1916), who in accepting the imperial dignity added to his name that of his great-great-uncle Joseph II, the famous enlightened reformer. As Francis Joseph I he was to rule the Habsburg Empire for sixty-eight years.

Though Prince Schwarzenberg was a confirmed enemy of constitutional liberalism and had no difficulty in guiding the young monarch in the same direction, the manifesto published at Francis Joseph's accession to the throne promised a constitutional rule. "Convinced on our own motion," it read, "of the need and value of free institutions expressive of the spirit of the age, we enter with due confidence on the path leading to a salutary transformation and the rejuvenation of the monarchy as a whole. On the basis of genuine liberty, on the basis of equality of all the nations of the realm and the equality before the law of all its citizens, and of participation of all those citizens in legislation, our Fatherland may enjoy a resurrection to its old greatness and a new vigor. Determined to maintain the splendor of the crown undimmed and the monarchy as a whole undiminished, but ready to share our rights with the representatives of our peoples, we count on succeeding, with the blessing of God and in understanding with all peoples, in uniting all the lands and races of the monarchy in one great state." The manifesto was an excellent declaration of intent. Wisely applied it might have preserved the monarchy. Unfortunately its letter and spirit did not correspond to the true intentions of the new government.

The Triumph of the Dynasty, 1849-50. Before being able to reëstablish absolutism, as it was Schwarzenberg's intention to do, Austria's authority had to be reestablished in Hungary, Italy, and Germany. This was a task accomplished in 1849 with apparent success. The most difficult situation was that faced in Hungary. There the Hungarian diet had worked out a constitution for the whole historical territory of the kingdom and this constitution became law on April 10, 1848. A ministry under Count Lajos Batthyány (1809-1849) was formed and was responsible to parliament. Serf labor, the tax exemption for the nobility, and the tithes for the clergy were abolished, and the freedom of the press was introduced. But the constitution failed lamentably to do what the Kremsier constitution did, to secure the equality and the free development of the various nationalities living in Hungary. (*See Reading No. 8.*) On the contrary, it subjected them to a process of ruthless Magyarization. Kossuth took the lead in rejecting all demands of the subject nationalities for concessions. This intransigent Magyar nationalism, which regarded the non-Magyar nationalists as in every respect inferior, not only contributed to the defeat of the liberal hopes of 1848 but doomed the growth of democracy in Hungary until 1918 and even beyond.

This Magyar intransigence aroused the resistance of the Rumanians, Slovaks, and Serbs. Their local revolts against Magyar domination were symptomatic but they were of little military importance. Different was the case of Croatia-Slavonia, where Count Josip Jelačić (1801-1859) was appointed Ban (governor-general) in March 1848. He convened a Croatian diet at Agram which put forward national and liberal demands. (*See Reading No. 7.*) Croatian forces crossed in September 1848 into Hungary proper and fought the Magyars. In January of the following year the Austrian army under Windischgrätz succeeded in occupying Budapest. The Hungarian diet withdrew to Debrecen in eastern Hungary, where on April 13 it proclaimed Hungary an independent republic (*see Reading No. 9*) and elected Kossuth "governor-president."

The Hungarian army, brilliantly led by General Arthur von Görgei (1818-1916) and supported by two Polish generals, József Bem (1795-1850) and Henryk Dembiński (1791-1864), resisted the Austrians under General Julius von Haynau (1786-1853) for some time but had to capitulate at Világos on August 13, when the Russian army invaded Hungary to support the Austrians. Two days before the surrender Kossuth had fled to Turkey. The Austrian command took cruel vengeance on the Hungarian military leaders. Thirteen generals were executed at Arad. The Habsburg rule was restored in Hungary.

Simultaneously with their victory in Hungary the Habsburgs restored their rule in Italy. The kingdom of Sardinia (Piedmont) renewed the war against Austria, in support of the Italians of Lombardy and Venetia, in March 1849, when events in Hungary seemed to offer an opportunity for the defeat of the Austrian army. But the Sardinians were again decisively defeated in the battle of Novara west of Milan in March, and in August, after a long siege, Venice surrendered to the Austrians and the short-lived republican regime there came to an end. At about the same time the Roman Republic proclaimed by Mazzini and Garibaldi in the Papal States fell to French troops. Mazzini was defeated as Kossuth was and both of them spent the rest of their lives in exile. The old order was reëstablished in 1849 throughout Italy. The Pope returned to Rome and the Habsburgs ruled again in Lombardy and Venetia. The aged Field Marshal Radetzky became governor-general of the two provinces.

Events in Germany took a similar turn. The German National Assembly in Frankfort offered in March 1849 the crown of a new German empire to the King of Prussia. He rejected it in April out of his deep hostility to any democratic or popular movement. It seemed to him unworthy to accept a crown from the hands of the elected representatives of the nation. His soldiers bloodily suppressed the German liberals who tried to continue the struggle for a democratic Germany. In the following year Prussia proposed a reform of the German Confederation, but Austria opposed this reform, which would have put an end to her leading position in the Confederation. In a conference held at Olmütz in November 1850 the Prussian government, partly under Russian pressure, had to accept the continuation of the German

Confederation under Austrian leadership. Thus by the end of 1850 the Habsburg Empire, under the vigorous leadership of Prince Schwarzenberg, reëstablished its leading position in Italy and Germany. It emerged from the stormy year of revolution apparently strengthened and its absolutist character restored. This development corresponded to a similar defeat of democracy and a similar glorification of absolute rule in revolutionary France. In the same month in which Francis Joseph ascended the throne of the Habsburgs, Louis Napoleon, the Bonapartist pretender to the imperial throne of France, was elected by an overwhelming majority of the French people president of the Second French Republic. In December 1851 he established his military dictatorship by a *coup d'état* and the following year he became Emperor of the French. In the same month of December 1851 the constitution, which had been granted in March 1849 but had never been put into force, was definitely suspended in Austria. Throughout the whole realm a strictly centralized and absolutist regime was established.

The reëstablishment of absolutism—and of a much more modern and efficient kind of absolutism than that before 1848 had been—demanded a strong personality at the head of the government. Prince Schwarzenberg, who was such a personality, died suddenly in April 1852. Among the men who had worked with him the strongest was Alexander Baron Bach (1813-1893), who as minister of the interior became responsible for a number of reforms abolishing ancient privileges and autonomies and increasing the efficiency of the administration. Though German was the language of administration and thus a unifying element of the Empire, no attempt was made to suppress the other nationalities. Such a system might have worked relatively well before 1848. But that year had aroused hopes for constitutional liberty among all the peoples of central Europe, and the Bach regime seemed to them a denial of political rights which they had come to expect as an indispensable element of modern times. The only relatively satisfied class were the peasants. The freedom which they had achieved in the

Revolution of 1848 remained unimpaired. But the fundamental test of the staying power of the absolutist regime did not come in its domestic policy but in the success or failure of its foreign policy.

— 3 —

THE END OF THE ERA
OF ABSOLUTISM

A Disastrous Foreign Policy. Throughout his reign Francis Joseph remained primarily concerned with foreign policy. He knew that he owed the survival of his dynasty in the crisis of 1848-49 to the army, and more than any of his predecessors he remained throughout his reign attached to it. He saw in it the chief bulwark and unifying factor of his regime. He felt himself to be, above all, a soldier. The regime was not militaristic, if by militarism we understand boastfulness and showmanship, as was the case in the France of Napoleon III and in the Germany of William II. Nor was there any interference of the army in the civilian departments of the government. Francis Joseph left these departments to the care of his ministers and adapted himself with ease and loyalty to the various future constitutional changes, proposed and carried through by his prime ministers. After 1867 he became a dutiful constitutional monarch and worked as hard and assiduously in the new framework of government as he had done in the old framework. At bottom Francis Joseph had no political or constitutional theories. His heart was not in domestic affairs. It was with his army and his foreign office.

After the death of Prince Schwarzenberg, Francis Joseph became for all practical purposes his own prime minister. The young man was in no way prepared for this difficult post nor did he find advisors who could have guided him. Within little more than a decade the position of Austria as a leading great power, which Schwarzenberg had restored, was lost. This was partly due to the fact that the economic and financial position of the Empire was overtaxed for the sake of the army. Very soon Francis Joseph had to face in the Prussian nobleman Otto von Bismarck, who in 1851 became the Prussian envoy to the Diet of the German Confederacy and in 1862 prime minister of Prussia, an adversary who equaled Schwarzenberg in energy and ruthlessness and surpassed him in political and diplomatic skill.

The oriental crisis of 1853 which brought Russia into conflict with Britain and France over the future of Turkey caused a deep estrangement between Francis Joseph and the Russian emperor Nicholas I, who had until then been extremely friendly to his younger fellow monarch. Francis Joseph's vacillating policy did not allow him to align himself either with Russia or with the Western Powers. During the Crimean War, Francis Joseph maintained a neutrality which as time went on appeared to be more and more unfriendly to Russia. For the sake of this armed neutrality the Austrian army remained mobilized, which caused a vast and ruinous expense. But it took no action. Thus it came about that the Austrian policy produced a lasting rift with Russia, where during the Crimean War Nicholas I died and was followed by his son Alexander II, and yet this policy did not win the friendship and confidence of the West. Thus Austria was left isolated in Europe. Napoleon III had offered a treaty of alliance to Austria during the war, but Francis Joseph rejected it. The British government, led by Palmerston, distrusted Austria out of sympathy for the Italian and Hungarian nationalists. Francis Joseph, who had tried to act as a mediator in the Crimean War between Russia on the one side and France and England on the other, found in the end "the late adversaries united in their dislike of the peacemaker." The great Austrian poet Grillparzer in his powerful historical tragedy *A Fraternal Conflict in the House of Habsburg* put the following words in the mouth of Emperor Matthias, who reigned from 1612 to 1619:

> This is a curse of Habsburg's noble house:
> Halfway to halt, and doubtfully to aim
> At half a deed, with half-considered means.

Such a curse followed Francis Joseph's policy in the great mid-century European crisis of the Crimean War.

More fortunate was the policy of the Sardinian Count Camillo Benso di Cavour who became in 1852 prime minister of his country and guided it for the next seven years. He concentrated on gaining Napoleon III's help in the struggle against Austria for the possession of Lombardy and Venetia. To that end he joined the French in the Crimean War. Napoleon III combined the traditional sympathy of his family for Italian aspirations with his new distrust of Francis Joseph, who had rejected the alliance proposed by the French Emperor. By the summer of 1858 he and Cavour had concluded a secret alliance for the expulsion of the Austrians from Italy. The maladroitness of Austrian diplomacy presented Sardinia with the long desired *casus belli,* making the Austrians appear as aggressors and assuring French support in the war which started in April 1859. Poorly led by Count Francis Gyulai (1798-1868) the Austrians missed the opportunity to defeat by an energetic advance the Sardinian army as they had done in 1848 and 1849 and were to do again in 1866. Instead the Austrians allowed the French army time to arrive in northern Italy. There the two armies met in June in the two indecisive battles of Magenta and Solferino. Both armies sustained very heavy losses, and this fact induced the two emperors, who were uncertain of the future, to conclude an armistice. In the peace treaty which followed, Austria ceded Lombardy to France, which gave it to Sardinia. But irrespective of the outcome of the war with Austria, Sardinia gained much more than Lombardy. Revolutionary agitations and actions in Italy itself, which were welcome neither to Francis Joseph nor to Napoleon, created within less than two years a united Italy under the Sardinian royal house. The Habsburgs retained only Venetia as a tenuous foothold in the Italian peninsula.

The Era of Constitutional Concessions. The failure of Austria's foreign policy created a disastrous financial position. At the same time, grave weaknesses in the armed forces themselves were revealed. Cases of corruption in the commissary department were reported and some Hungarian and Italian troops proved unreliable. Bach was dismissed as minister of the interior. A new constitution was hastily worked out and imposed in October 1860, only to be radically changed again in February 1861. These constitutions in spite of their illiberal character, revived political life and started political discussion anew. One fundamental difficulty was presented by the fact that the Austrian Germans strove for a more or less unitary monarchy, whereas the Magyars insisted, not on the decentralization or federalization of the empire, which would have been salutary, but on the separateness of a strictly unitary and centralized Hungarian kingdom from the rest of the monarchy.

The constitution of 1861, drawn up under the influence of Anton Ritter von Schmerling (1805-1893) emphasized the unitary character of the Habsburg Empire with German preponderance, but satisfied neither the nationalities nor the liberals. It did not introduce a parliamentary system nor did it establish full constitutional liberties. The Hungarians were in open opposition to the new constitution from the beginning. Their leaders were now Ferencz Deák (1803-1876) and Count Gyula Andrássy (1823-1890). Differing from Kossuth, they realized that Hungary could exist and thrive only in connection with the Habsburg Empire, but they were also convinced that within a loose common framework Hungary must retain and develop her historical personality. In a famous article which appeared in the Easter issue of *Pesti Napló* on April 16, 1865, Deák declared Hungary's willingness to harmonize her historical right with the necessary conditions which would make possible the position of the Habsburg Empire as a whole as a great power. His proposals became the foundation of the new constitutional arrangements which later entered into power, but not before a further interlude of an unfortunate foreign policy had lost to the Habsburgs their traditional position in Germany as well as in Italy.

Austria and Prussia in 1866. The year 1866 was a decisive year in the history of central Europe, of Germany as a whole and of the Habsburg monarchy. For Germany it meant the establishment of Prussian domina-

tion over all the smaller German states and the final
unification, not by democratic parliamentary procedure
but by the victories of the Prussian army and by the
adroit diplomacy of Bismarck, Prussia's prime minister.
For the Habsburg monarchy it meant exclusion from
Germany, where the Habsburgs had played the most
prominent role among the princely dynasties for almost
six hundred years, and the transformation of the Austrian
monarchy into an Austrian-Hungarian monarchy, a political construction without parallel in history. The year
1866 brought the triumph of German and Magyar nationalism at the expense of the other peoples of central
Europe. It prevented a truly federal solution, which had
been sought since 1848 and which might have preserved
the area of central Europe from the ravages of an exaggerated and self-centered nationalism that was growing
among all its peoples until it produced the catastrophes
of the twentieth century.

By 1863 Austria under Francis Joseph and Prussia
under its new king, William I, started to compete openly
for leadership in the German Confederation. Both princes
represented conservative and traditionalist monarchies.
But Prussia understood better how to harness the modern trend of nationalism and of middle-class support for
its purpose. More disastrous for Francis Joseph, however, was the fact that he had no advisor of the intellectual superiority and astuteness of a Bismarck. Surrounded by mediocrities, the Austrian Emperor repeated
again the vacillating policy which had defeated him in
1859. He allowed himself to be drawn into the war with
Denmark in 1864 under conditions which were advantageous for Prussia and disadvantageous for Austria, and
his diplomatic maneuvering in the first part of 1866
brought him neither the support of Napoleon III nor of
Italy. Bismarck, on the other hand, concluded an alliance with Italy and was ready to use Magyar and Czech
nationalism as weapons to subvert the Habsburg position.

The war which Prussia entered in June 1866 was not
a war against Austria alone but a war against the German
Confederation. All the major members of this confederation fought on Austria's side. On the other hand, Prussia

was supported by Italy, though Austria had promised, in
return for French neutrality, to cede Venetia to Napoleon, who was to retrocede it to Italy, whether Austria won or lost the war. In fact, though Austria had to
concentrate most of her army in the north against Prussia, she was able to defeat the Italians with great ease,
both on land and at sea. The Austrian army under Archduke Albrecht (1817-1895) won the battle of Custoza,
and the Austrian navy under Admiral Wilhelm von
Tegetthoff (1827-1871) defeated the superior Italian
force near Lissa, a Dalmatian island (now called Vis).

Different was the development in the north, where the
Prussian and the combined Austrian and Saxon armies
met on July 3 near Königgrätz (Hradec Králové) in
eastern Bohemia. The Austrian army was led by Ludwig
August von Benedek (1804-1881), a gifted officer who
had accepted the command on the unfamiliar Bohemian
terrain only under protest and had been poorly assisted
by his staff. The Prussian infantry, using a much more
modern rifle, had a great superiority over the Austrians.
Nevertheless, the latter had the better of the day-long
battle until the afternoon, when the arrival of the second
Prussian army decided the outcome—not only the outcome of the battle but also the outcome of the war and
the future of central Europe.

Three weeks later, on July 26, the preliminary peace
was concluded. Prussia annexed several German states,
but the conditions imposed upon Austria were, upon Bismarck's insistence, not too heavy. The German Confederation created in 1815 was terminated and Austria was
excluded from participation in German affairs. Thus the
summer of 1866 ended the centuries-old role of the Habsburgs in Germany and in Italy.

A few years later, on January 18, 1871, Prussia established on the battlefields of France the new German
Empire. Bismarck became the adored hero of German
nationalism and he and his empire began to exercise a
great attraction for many Germans in the Habsburg Empire. Bismarck himself, however, always opposed the
demands of the Austrian Germans for union (*Anschluss*)
with the German Reich which he had established with

Berlin as its center. He regarded the continuation of the Habsburg monarchy, with its strong German element, as indispensable for Germany's power position in Europe. He was therefore ready not only to support the preservation of the Habsburg monarchy but to enter into an alliance with it. For this alliance Bismarck relied for support not only on the Germans in the Habsburg monarchy but even more upon the Magyars. For one of the consequences of the year 1866 and of Austria's defeat in the war against Prussia was the transformation of the Austrian monarchy into the Austro-Hungarian monarchy, in which the Magyars played a dominant role far beyond their numerical, cultural, or economic strength.

The two main results of the fateful year of 1866—the Reich which Bismarck established under Prussian leadership and the Austro-Hungarian or Dual Monarchy —lasted for about half a century. Both perished in World War I, which was brought about largely as a result of their structure and spirit and thus, too, can be regarded as an outcome of the turn which history took in and after 1866.

The Dual Monarchy. After the defeat of 1866 the future of the Habsburg Empire was settled in negotiations between Andrássy, the adroit spokesman of the Magyar nobility, and Count Friedrich Ferdinand von Beust (1809-1886), who had been Saxony's leading statesman and who in October 1866 became Austrian foreign minister. Hungary received within her historical frontiers constitutional independence. The other parts of the Habsburg Empire and the non-Magyar nationalities in the Hungarian kingdom were not consulted. The settlement of 1867 established the exclusive rule of the Magyars in the kingdom of Hungary and the preponderance of Hungary within what had now become the Dual Monarchy. Francis Joseph was from now on Emperor of Austria and King of Hungary. But the union between these two parts was no longer a purely personal one, as the Hungarian constitution of 1848 had demanded. There was a common monarchy which included the two affairs closest to the monarch's heart, the army and the foreign policy. Hungary received a parliamentary constitution based on a suffrage and on a practice of election which excluded the lower classes and the non-Magyar nationalities from any share in the government.

Nevertheless, Hungary represented a well-organized and historical entity. That was not the case with the rest of the Habsburg Empire. It was sometimes called Austria, but the name was also sometimes used for the whole of the Dual Monarchy, known also as Austro-Hungary. Officially the non-Hungarian parts of the Habsburg Empire were known as "the kingdoms and lands represented in the Reichstag" (the German name for the parliament). The relation between the two parts of the Habsburg Empire was governed by two laws officially accepted by the two parts. (*See Reading No. 10.*) The executive power for affairs common to the whole monarchy was exercised by the Emperor, who reserved to himself exclusively the management, conduct, and internal organization of the army, and by three ministers, one for foreign affairs, one for the army, and one for finances with reference to matters of common expense. The legislative power was exercised by means of delegations from the legislative bodies of the two parts of the Empire. In these delegations Hungary counted for as much as all the other provinces put together; and being a much more unified body, she counted for much more. In addition to the common affairs (army and foreign policy) the following matters which were not administered in common were regulated upon uniform principles to be agreed upon every ten years by a "compromise" (*Ausgleich*): customs legislation, certain indirect taxes, a common monetary system, and railway lines affecting the interests of both parties.

In this compromise Francis Joseph surrendered practically everything to Magyar aspirations except the army and foreign affairs. The Magyars were less generous in their settlement with Croatia-Slavonia which was concluded in 1868. Croatia-Slavonia retained her own Diet (*Sabor*) and the right to use her own language, but there was no responsible ministry and the governor was appointed by the Hungarian ministry. The harbor city of

Fiume, which was geographically and ethnically in Croat territory, was transferred to Hungary.

More important was the new constitution for the western part of the Empire, which from now on will be called Austria. There was an attempt to organize Austria on federal lines, but it was frustrated by Magyar opposition, based on the fear that a federal nationality policy in Austria could influence developments in Hungary and thus put an end to Magyar rule there. The Magyars hoped that Austria would be ruled in similar way by the Germans, and that the Poles of Galicia, to whom the large Ukrainian population of that province would be abandoned, would form the third of the three master races of the Dual Monarchy. But the Austrian constitution, published on December 31, 1867, did not fulfill Magyar hopes. It laid the foundations for a much more liberal state than Hungary was. Article XIX of the Austrian constitution recognized equality of the Austrian nationalities and the rights of each nationality to preserve its language.

The new constitution contained also an extensive bill of rights. Though the franchise was at the beginning very limited and construed in such a way as to give to the Germans a much larger share than their numbers warranted, the property qualifications of the franchise were repeatedly lowered, until in 1907 equal and democratic voting rights were established. The constitution recognized the principle of ministerial responsibility and introduced a strong guarantee of judicial independence. Individual rights were safeguarded by the establishment of the *Reichsgericht,* a supreme court of public and administrative laws. Thus by the end of 1867 the Austrian part of the Habsburg Empire had entered the road to modern constitutionalism. The era of monarchical absolutism was ended, and no attempt was made to restore it. But the fundamental problem of the Habsburg Empire, as it emerged into the age of nationalism, remained unsolved.

The Dual Monarchy represented a unique and very complex governmental structure (*see Reading No. 11*), which became even more complex in 1878 when the

Turkish province of Bosnia-Herzegovina was added to
the monarchy. There were three different cabinets, one
for Austria, one for Hungary, and one for common
affairs. To maintain this complex structure against the
ever-growing encroachments of the Magyars was the
difficult task performed by Francis Joseph in the last fifty
years of his life. Under Deák's leadership the Magyars,
and that means the ruling oligarchy, had shown a sense
of moderation. "We must not overrate our strength,"
Deák had said, "and must confess that on our own we
are not a great state." But Deák died in 1876 and then
the overweening nationalism of Kossuth prevailed and
led to a catastrophe which buried not only the Dual Monarchy but the proud historical kingdom of Hungary itself.

One of the leading Austrian political scientists, Joseph
Redlich, saw Francis Joseph after 1867 "toiling to maintain his dual realm, forever devising new expedients for
upholding the institutions and the forms of the pro-
Hungarian 1867 constitution, while around him there
gathers all the time the mounting tide of resistance by
all the other nationalities to the intolerable, unjust, and
untenable predominance of the Magyar race. In its
strangeness, in its tension, in its tragedy, here is a drama
unparalleled in contemporary European history."

— 4 —

THE QUEST FOR AN AUSTRIAN IDEA

An Empire Without an Idea. Francis Joseph, who came more and more to represent the unity of the Habsburg Empire until in his late age he became its foremost symbol, had only one goal, to preserve the Empire. In a way he was the last traditional monarch who believed that dynastic ties and interests could suffice as the basis of a nation as they did in the eighteenth century. Like a good eighteenth-century monarch, he regarded himself as the first servant of the nation, but he identified the nation with himself and his dynasty. He worked indefatigably for the good of his people, but they were *his* people and *he* interpreted what was good for them. In the eighteenth century his reign would have been considered, on the whole, a good one. In the later nineteenth century, in the era of the awakening of the peoples, his reign suffered from a complete lack of ideas, from a starved imagination.

Yet such an idea could have been developed. The Austrian poet Hugo von Hofmannsthal (1874-1929) in 1917 wrote an essay called "The Austrian Idea" in which he called Austria the conciliator and mediator between the Latin-Germanic world of the European West and the Byzantine and Slavic worlds in the East. This Austrian *raison d'être* was obscured after 1848 by the growth of nationalism. The American historian John Lothrop Motley, who was his country's minister to Vienna in the 1860's, remarked then that "the problem how to create a nation out of nationalities, . . . an empire out of provinces and states is as old as history, and one of the most difficult and most important for human sagacity to solve."

Unfortunately, Austria was unable to solve the problem. Many of its influential citizens saw Austria as a German outpost for the control and order of central Europe, not as a supranational European factor. Yet, the formation of the monarchy, with its deep roots in the past, as well as its growth had not been conditioned or made possible as part of Germany but by its orientation towards the other peoples and kingdoms of the Danubian Basin and of Europe in general. Austria was not a German frontier march; it was a bridge on which Germany and Europe met and where all European civilizations mingled in mutual stimulation. Under these circumstances it behooved Austria to show tolerance and moderation, to avoid extremes, to permeate its life with a broad-minded catholicity and a strong tendency to ease the living together of different types, languages, and races. But this even temper was threatened in the nineteenth century by the aggressiveness of German and Magyar nationalism from which the other peoples learned, just as it had been in the seventeenth century by the burning intolerance of the Spanish Counter Reformation.

A German historian, Onno Klopp, who after the annexation of his native Hanover in 1866 came to live in Vienna, complained bitterly how little the Austrian authorities cared about an understanding, on the part of the population, of the idea or the history of the Austrian state. "All feeling for a common purpose is missing here," he wrote. "It is terrible to think out the consequences. A power which has only to expect moral strength and advantages from the historical presentation of its principles, not only does not promote such a presentation, but hinders it." The eighteenth-century conservative imperial structure was indifferent to public opinion and was adverse to modern propaganda and publicity. Thus it became distant and aloof from the political life of the peoples and formed a close society outside the main stream of modern social and cultural movements. It disdainfully abstained from demagogy and from wooing the new rising classes; it avoided the vulgarity of late nineteenth-century ostentatiousness and of mass communication. But for that reason it got out of touch with the people, who were more and more preoccupied with their own aspirations, and succumbed to nationalist demagogy.

The Austrian Idea Seen by a Czech. An Austrian idea in the age of nationalism would have necessitated the transformation of the whole Habsburg Empire into a monarchical federation of peoples living on a footing of equality and developing autonomously their national culture but cooperating closely in the common concern for national security, for the maintenance of peace, and for economic growth. Such had been the program of the constitution drawn up at Kremsier in 1849. The Czech national leader Palacký had backed this program and remained fundamentally faithful to it throughout his life, though after the Compromise with Hungary he despaired of his realization. "We Czechs certainly wish sincerely the preservation and unity of Austria," he wrote at the approach of the negotiations leading to the Compromise and disregarding the interest of the Czechs. "Considering that by our own efforts we could scarcely create an independent sovereign state, we can preserve our historico-political entity, our particular nationality and culture, and finally, our economic life nowhere and in no way better than we can in Austria. That means in a free Austria organized on the basis of autonomy and equality. We have no hopes and no political perspectives beyond Austria; we have no conationals and fellow people sharing our language in the narrower sense of the concept. Should anybody say we are friends of Austria only out of egotism, we would agree readily. Politicians, who are not naïve, will admit that such friends used to be the most faithful and reliable ones."

Palacký's most important disciple, the philosopher and sociologist Thomas Garrigue Masaryk (1850-1937) who later became the first president of the Czechoslovakian republic wrote of Palacký after World War I: "My guide and master was Palacký, the father of the fatherland, who gave us a philosophical history of our nation, understood its place in the world, and defined our national objective." It was one of the fundamental political conceptions of Palacký, Masaryk wrote, that the Czech people could not become politically independent. "As regards the relation of the Czech lands to the Austrian state," Masaryk asserted as late as 1895 in his most important programmatic book on The Czech Question, "I regard Palacký's idea of the Austrian state, in spite of all constitutional changes, as a still reliable guide: it is regrettable, that Palacký . . . himself abandoned to a certain degree his idea and recommended a more Slav national program; thereby he has unwittingly strengthened the political phantasts. . . . I act according to his program when I express my political experiences in the words, that our policy cannot be successful if it is not supported by a true and strong interest in the fate of Austria, . . . by the cultural and political effort to work in harmony with the needs of our people for the advancement of the whole of Austria and its political administration."

Masaryk stressed that Palacký regarded as the foremost concrete political goal for the Czechs to establish a liberal relationship with the Bohemian Germans, "who have inhabited Bohemia jointly with us since the oldest time." Palacký believed in the desirability of an Austrian federation as a protective shield against Pan-Germanism and Pan-Russianism, and within this Austrian federation he hoped for a Bohemian federation of the Slav Czech nation with part of the German people. Unfortunately this liberal solution was not achieved, neither in the Habsburg empire, when German and Magyar nationalism prevented its realization, nor in the Czechoslovak republic, when Czech nationalism prevented it.

In his "The Idea of the Austrian State" Palacký warned in 1865 against the coming Compromise with Hungary, against the creation of a dual monarchy at the expense of the other nationalities. "I am convinced that the dualism in any form whatsoever will prove within not too long a time destructive for the whole monarchy, more destructive than a complete centralization would be." He demanded "that the Austrian government should be neither German, nor Magyar, nor Slav, nor Latin, but Austrian in a higher and general sense, that means on the basis of equal justice for all its members. . . . That more than three hundred years ago such different peoples have by free agreements formed the Austrian Empire, I regard as no small blessing of providence for all of them. If it had not happened and if each of these peoples had kept its full sovereign rights, in how many and how bloody struggles would they have faced each other during that time! Perhaps some of them might even have perished."

The Austrian Idea as Seen by a German. One of the Austrian-German liberals who was not deflected from his liberalism by the upsurge of nationalism was Adolf Fischhof (1816-1893), a physician who took an active part in the Revolution of 1848 and in the Kremsier Parliament. Joseph Redlich called him "both personally and politically one of the noblest and most significant figures ever produced by Austrian democracy." In 1869 he published *Austria and the Guarantees of Its Existence* in which he demanded the recognition that Austria must be a federal state, a *Völkerstaat*. He pleaded for decentralization and autonomy not only because the Habsburg Empire embraced different nationalities, but also because he clearly recognized that in countries with strong local self-government, such as the United States, Britain, and Switzerland, civic freedom was safe. In Austria's case there was an added reason for a reorganization on the basis of autonomy. Fischhof was convinced that if the Austrian-Slav peoples enjoyed a safe status of national development and property, there would be little danger of a Russia-centered Pan-Slavism. In a letter, quoted by Redlich, Fischhof protested against the expansionist policy in the Balkans being pursued by the Austrian government under its foreign minister Andrássy, who was the chief architect of the Austro-German alliance and of the occupation of Bosnia-Herzegovina.

"A sound eastern policy," Fischhof wrote, "is possible only on the basis of a rational domestic policy, noninjurious to the Slav peoples, since the eastern question is a predominantly Slav one. Pan-Slavism can be overcome only by opposing it with a sound idea, not by mobilizing great armies. The Pan-Slav bait could best be counteracted by reasonable encouragement to the various Slav local nationalisms." Criticizing the reliance upon the alliance with Bismarckian Germany, Fischhof wrote: "In the long run it is not an alliance of princes, nor an entente cordiale of diplomats that will help us, but unity at home and the friendly cooperation of all the nationalities that make up our state, for the chasms that divide our nationalities will one day be the grave of the monarchy."

Another Austrian liberal, Franz Schuselka (1811-1886) of Bohemian-German origin, fought in his weekly *Die Reform,* which he published from 1852 to 1879, for a federal Austria. He understood that an overemphasis on national rights threatened to frustrate the ideas of liberty and humanity. "In Austria," he wrote, "no people should rule over another and least of all over all other peoples. All peoples must enjoy equal rights, which will result in the voluntary fulfilment of common duties. Austria must be conceived as a multinational state, it must be so constituted that it does not absorb any nationality but preserves all. To that end, Austria was created; in this end lies the justification of its continued existence." His idea of a *Völkerreich,* a multinational state, ran counter to the dominant aspirations for creating exclusive nation-states. This aspiration was represented in its most extreme form by the Magyars in Hungary, but it was equally dominant in the succession states which emerged out of the liquidation of the Habsburg Empire in 1918, in Poland, in Czechoslovakia, in Yugoslavia, and in Rumania. The central European nation-states, which turned many of their citizens into second-class citizens on account of their nationality and later went even so far as to expel the inhabitants of a territory for the same reason, facilitated in our own days the establishment of totalitarian control over central-eastern Europe. Against the danger of an expansive Pan-Slavism led by Russia Schuselka warned as early as 1849. Russia, he wrote, was animated by an ideological enthusiasm and by the nationalist fantasy of uniting all Slav nations into a great world empire. She was not satisfied with theoretical enthusiasm. "She works with confident faith and

therefore with unbreakable perseverance for the practical realization of her enthusiasm. . . . An attempt to
realize Pan-Slavism would seriously threaten Austria's
existence."

The Crown Prince and the Austrian Idea. The
opposition to the Emperor's policy or to his lack of an
imaginative policy did not come merely from a few middle-class writers who insisted that only a federal transformation could preserve the empire in the interests of
all its citizens and of international peace. The official
policy of avoiding all risks in order to preserve the fragile
order which existed was also opposed from circles near-
est to the throne. In 1854 Francis Joseph married a Bavarian princess, Elizabeth (1837-1898), who combined
great beauty with a lively interest, unknown at Francis
Joseph's court, in modern literature and movements.
Their only son Rudolf (1858-1889) inherited his mother's
cultural interests as well as her high-strung personality.
Very well educated in many fields, gifted and of great
personal charm, he wished to open up a new era of Austria's future which he felt threatened by his father's timid
and conservative policy. His political aspirations drove
him into opposition to the court. He was in sympathy
with the liberal and scientific outlook of modern times;
he was personally a friend of liberal journalists who, like
all journalists, were kept far away from court circles,
and an admirer of the Third French Republic and of
personalities like Léon Gambetta. He was animated by
the impatience of a brilliant and erratic youth and by
that of a son who thinks that his father wastes his in-
heritance. He combined his late nineteenth-century liberalism with a deep faith in Austria's future and an aggressive imperialism which did not shy away from the
possibility of wars with Russia and Italy in order to for-
tify Austria's position in the Balkans. In domestic policy
he regarded nationalism as a reactionary and atavistic
movement and favored a cosmopolitan supranational liberal policy.

Rudolf had not the time to develop his frequently
conflicting and incongruous ideas into a workable whole.
The unhappy marriage which he concluded in 1881,

largely at the demand of his father, with Stephanie, the seventeen-year-old daughter of King Leopold II of Belgium, increased his restlessness. To affirm the Austrian idea he published, in twenty-four volumes, a richly illustrated survey of the Habsburg Empire, *Die Österreichisch-Ungarische Monarchie in Wort und Bild* (The Austrian-Hungarian Monarchy in Word and Image). He was too proud as an Austrian and too liberal in his thought not to resent Austria's dependence on the reactionary Berlin regime. But he never matured enough to take reality fully into account. In some ways he resembled the great eighteenth-century enlightened Habsburg, Joseph II. His tragic position as a crown prince who consumes his energies in vain hopes of actions led him into a personal and political impasse. Suicide, the immediate motives and circumstances of which were never completely resolved, put an end to his life in the hunting lodge of Meyerling near Vienna. He was then in his thirty-first year.

The Last Quest for an Austrian Idea. Rudolf's suicide and the death of Archduke Karl Ludwig (1833-1896), brother of Francis Joseph, made Karl's son Franz Ferdinand (1863-1914) the successor to the throne. In many respects he was the very opposite of Rudolf. While the latter was a liberal who opposed the Church and the nobility, Franz Ferdinand was deeply conservative, devoted to Catholicism and to the feudal aristocracy. He was happily married to Sophie Countess Chotek of a noble Czech family, whom he chose as a wife against the strongest opposition of the court and for whose sake, because she was not of royal blood, he had to renounce the right to succession for their progeny. But both princes had much in common: the contradictory nature of their plans, their complex character, and their dedication to see a strong and rejuvenated Austria animated by the sense of a mission. Franz Ferdinand had neither Rudolf's personal charm nor his broad education. But he had more solid backing and the advice of more mature and competent men. He hoped to strengthen the cohesive forces of the Empire by revising the Compromise of 1867, by ending the oppression of the non-Magyar nationalities in Hungary with a democratic extension of the vote, and by conceding some of the demands of the non-German nationalities in Austria.

Unlike Rudolf, Franz Ferdinand shied away from military adventures and understood that the Austrian Empire needed peace. Though he wished to satisfy the nationalities of the Habsburg Empire, he did so not out of an understanding of modern national aspirations but in order to strengthen the Habsburg crown. He profoundly regretted that the times of feudalism and absolutism had passed. He was out of tune with the new rising forces of the time. Thus his project of reviving Austria by a consciousness of a mission and idea would have probably failed even if a tragic fate had not cut short his life as it did that of Rudolf. On June 28, 1914, Franz Ferdinand and his wife were assassinated by a Serb patriot-terrorist. Their death precipitated the Great War and the disintegration of the empire which Franz Ferdinand had striven to preserve.

— 5 —

THE STRUGGLE OF THE NATIONALITIES

The Development in Hungary. The disintegration of the Habsburg Empire was caused primarily by the growing struggle of nationalities for the fulfillment of their aspirations. In 1867 Hungary had a population of about thirteen and a half million, of whom only six million were Magyars. The original nationality law of 1868, drafted by Baron József Eötvös (1813-1871) a liberal statesman and then minister of public education, opposed federalism but wished to satisfy those claims of ethnic or linguistic nationalism which were compatible with the continuation and strengthening of the historical and political entity of the Hungarian kingdom. The law recognized the rights of the languages of the various nationalities in elementary and secondary schools and their use on the lower levels of administration. But this nationality law was never enforced in the relatively liberal spirit in which it was established. Though the party formed by the Magyar gentry which ruled Hungary after Deák's death called itself the Liberal Party, it represented the most narrow nationality and class interests. Deák himself warned in his speech in the Hungarian parliament in 1872 that intolerance in the nationality problem would ultimately endanger the Magyars themselves, as fifty years later it did. The harsh territorial conditions imposed upon Hungary in the peace treaty in 1919 can be explained in the light of the ferocious persecutions to which the non-Magyar nationalities were subjected in the Hungarian kingdom.

It must be stressed, however, that this policy of Magyar supremacy was not a racial policy. It did not aim at the extinction or expulsion of the non-Magyars but at their assimilation, or rather the assimilation of their leading classes. If they accepted the Magyar language and culture, if they showed an inclination to abandon their nationality and mother tongue, they were accepted as equals and given their share in the spoils of the regime. But those who wished to develop their Slovak, Rumanian, Croatian, or Ukrainian nationalities and languages were fiercely repressed. Therein the Liberal Party was in complete agreement with the even more radical Magyar National Independence Party, which was under the leadership of Kossuth's son Ferenc (1841-1914). Kossuth's party wished to loosen completely the ties with Austria, whereas the Liberal Party under the leadership of Kálmán Tisza (1830-1902), who was prime minister from 1875 to 1890, and of his son István (1861-1918), who was prime minister from 1903 to 1905 and from 1913 to 1917, was willing to uphold the Compromise with Austria, but wished to modify it every ten years more and more in favor of Hungary and to assure Hungary the preponderant voice in the Habsburg Empire.

The word "Hungary" in this connection meant the ruling oligarchy. It excluded, on the strength of a very limited franchise, not only the non-Magyar nationalities which formed the majority of the population but also the Magyar lower classes, above all the peasants, who continued to live in the abject poverty typical of underdeveloped feudal countries. In 1900, ten million out of thirteen million of the farm population owned no land whatsoever. Less than one-fifth of 1 per cent of the landowners owned large estates of more than one thousand acres, covering about one-third of the whole area. Owing to its low productivity, Hungarian agriculture suffered from the competition of overseas grain, and this notwithstanding the high natural fertility of the soil in the Danubian plain.

This combination of extreme injustice from the nationality as well as from the social point of view made it possible for the Crown to use the threat of introducing universal suffrage to restrain the majority of the parliament which demanded the loosening of the ties with Austria. In their conflict with the Crown, the Magyar leaders had hoped that the people would rise in defense of the traditional constitution, which was regarded as something sacred. Yet not only the non-Magyar nationalities but the Magyar peasants and workers too remained entirely indifferent. On the other hand, the Socialists were able to organize a mass demonstration in Budapest, the country's capital, in October 1907 in favor of electoral reform. The threat of such a reform induced the ruling oligarchy to abandon its demands for loosening the ties with Austria and for the Magyarization of the army. The crown having achieved its purpose abandoned its sponsorship of universal suffrage, which meanwhile had been introduced in the Austrian part of the Empire.

Thus Hungary was unwilling and unable to solve its nationality and its social problems before 1918. The Electoral Law of 1874 not only restricted the franchise to about 800,000 persons, but excluded the non-Magyars practically from the vote by a very uneven distribution of electoral areas, by a highly complicated franchise, and by voting by public declaration which made it easy for the Magyar government officials to intimidate voters. The subject nationalities in Hungary suffered not only from their exclusion from participation in government administration, but also from neglect of their education. It may be sufficient to mention the case of the more than two million Slovaks in northwestern Hungary. The Slovak cultural organization which promoted Slovak education and literature, the Slovenská Matica, was dissolved in 1875. In the same year Prime Minister Tisza declared in the Hungarian parliament that no Slovak nationality existed. In 1875 there were in Slovakia 1,805 elementary schools in which Slovak was taught besides Magyar; in 1905 only 241 of these schools were in existence. The Slovak teachers were carefully selected and closely supervised by the local Magyar authorities. At the end of the nineteenth century there was only one Slovak newspaper published in Hungary. In spite of these repressive measures, the national consciousness of the non-Magyar nationalities in Hungary grew throughout the latter part of the nineteenth century, in conformity with the general trend of the time.

The Development in Galicia. The Carpathian Mountains separated Galicia from Hungary. The Poles who formed the leading nationality in Galicia felt ties of sympathy and of a similarity of fundamental attitudes with the Magyars, the ruling nationality in Hungary. In Galicia the Poles formed the majority of the population and were much superior in economic wealth, social prestige, and educational opportunities to the Ukrainians, who represented more than 40 per cent of the population. In one respect Poles and Ukrainians were in similar situations. The Poles were not, like the Magyars, the Czechs, or the Slovaks, confineu to Austria. The majority lived outside the Austrian borders, in Russia and in Prussia. Most Ukrainians also lived outside Galicia; their vast majority was in Russia, and smaller groups were in the Austrian province of Bucovina and on the southern (Hungarian) slopes of the Carpathian Mountains. Conditions in Galicia resembled rather those in Hungary than those in the more progressive Austrian lands. Economically and socially, Galicia was underdeveloped and the Polish nobility and gentry occupied there a position similar to that of the corresponding Magyar classes in Hungary. But thanks to the system prevailing in Austria after 1867, the position of the lower classes in Galicia never became as desperate as in Hungary, and the national rights of the Ukrainian minority were never disregarded in the same way as were the rights of the non-Magyar nationalities in Hungary.

After the Compromise of 1867 the position of the Poles in the Austrian monarchy improved rapidly, not only in comparison with the oppression which the Poles in Russia and Prussia suffered but even considered by itself. In 1868 Galicia received, largely at the expense of the Ukrainians, a broad measure of administrative home rule, in exchange for which the Polish conservatives supported the Austrian government. For all practical purposes Galicia was administered by the Poles themselves; at the same time Polish noblemen like Count

Agenor Goluchowski (1812-1875) and his son of the same name (1849-1921) played a great role in imperial affairs; the latter was Austro-Hungarian foreign minister from 1895 to 1906. In Galicia the Poles had also all the facilities of free cultural development which were refused to them in Russia and Prussia. The Polish University of Cracow (Kraków), where the Polish kings were crowned and buried until 1764, was one of the oldest universities of Europe, having been founded in 1364. The Poles also had an Institute of Technology and a second university in Lemberg (called Lwów in Polish and Lwiw in Ukrainian), the largest city in the eastern or Ukrainian part of Galicia. This university was founded under Joseph II in 1784, its languages of instruction being at that time Latin and German. Polish became the language of instruction there in 1871, and only later lectures were given in Ukrainian too. Among the Ukrainians in Galicia there was a strong current which looked for salvation in union with Russia.

The Development in Bohemia. Bohemia, and to a lesser extent neighboring Moravia, formed the classic battleground between Slav and German nationalisms. There, according to Professor Joseph Redlich, "the forms and methods, the whole technique, psychology, and procedure of the modern national struggle of civilized nations were developed. Here the whole phenomenon of nationalism fully evolved for the first time in its boundless ideological and psychological effects." The conflict between the Czechs and the Germans in Bohemia was not merely an Austrian problem. Behind the Germans in Bohemia and Moravia stood the power of the Germans in the old Austrian hereditary lands and in the German Empire—a power which might be vaguely called Pan-Germanism; behind the Czechs stood the sympathy of Russia, the largest Slav nation, a sympathy which might be vaguely called Pan-Slavism. The struggle between Czechs and Germans for predominance in Bohemia was one of the causes which led to the disintegration of the Habsburg Empire. It was later the principal cause which led to the collapse of the Czechoslovak Republic. The struggle which began in the first part of the nineteenth century, with the dawn of the age of nationalism in central Europe, gained in intensity, because after 1867 the Czechs, favored by the more liberal climate in Austria, made extraordinary gains in the cultural and in the economic field. Bohemia differed fundamentally from Hungary and Galicia. There the decisive factors were the Magyar and the Polish nobility; in Bohemia it was a new and quickly rising Czech middle class which transformed Bohemia into a socially and economically much more developed and "western" part of central Europe than Hungary or Galicia were.

The development of Czech literature remained largely unknown abroad, but Czech music was widely recognized. Bedřich Smetana (1824-1884) wrote a number of operas of which *The Bartered Bride* (1866) became the most popular, while *Libussa,* celebrating the first legendary queen of Bohemia, opened the first Czech National Theater in 1868. When this theater burned down, the Czechs built a more magnificent one. All the financial resources for it came from private donations collected by the people; accordingly the theater, which opened in 1883, bore the proud inscription "The People to Itself." Smetana wrote also a sequence of six symphonic poems *My Fatherland* describing the loveliness of the homeland and its heroic past. A younger Czech composer, Antonín Dvořák (1841-1904), spent some time as a conductor in the United States, a period of his life which was reflected in his *New World Symphony*.

Czech intellectual life was stimulated by the creation in 1882 of a Czech university, where Masaryk became professor of philosophy. An organization called Matice promoted the publication of popular books and helped to establish Czech schools. After the example of the German gymnastic associations (Turnerschaften) a similar Czech organization under the name Sokol ("the falcon") was founded. The earlier leading political party, the Old Czechs led by Palacký and his son-in-law Rieger, gave way, with the progressive democratization and radicalization of Czech national life, to the Young Czech Party, which founded the first really modern and metropolitan newspaper in Prague *Národní Listy* (National

Newspaper), in 1861 and was later led by Karel Kramář (1860-1937).

The efforts of the Austrian governments under Prime Minister Count Eduard Taaffe (1833-1895), a Bohemian nobleman of Irish descent, and Count Kasimir Badeni (1846-1909), a Polish nobleman from Galicia, to bring about an agreement between the Czechs and the Germans failed. Taaffe was prime minister from 1879 to 1893 and strove, as he declared in his program, for "a reconciliation of the nationalities." Badeni, who was prime minister from 1895 to 1897, attempted to place the Czech language on a par with the German language in Bohemia and Moravia. Their efforts were frustrated by Magyar and German opposition. The result was that Czech and German nationalism (especially among the Germans in Bohemia for whom later the term Sudeten Germans was used) became more and more embittered. The democratization of the suffrage in the Austrian parliament gave the Czech masses a growing strength. The rapid development of industry in the predominantly German districts in northern Bohemia attracted many Czech workers from the predominantly agrarian parts in the center of the country. As a result the numerical proportion in the population figures of the nationalities shifted in favor of the Czechs. The conflict grew so bitter that Bohemian politics were filled with much fuss about petty questions of the use of the Czech or German language on street signs and menus in restaurants.

Thus the foundations were laid for the tragic developments of the twentieth century. Many Bohemian Germans insisted on treating Bohemia as a part of Germany, appealing to the past for a justification when the king of Bohemia had been one of the Electors of the Holy Roman Empire and later the Bohemian lands formed part of the German Confederation. The Czechs on their side appealed similarly to the past, insisting on the "Bohemian State right" of the "crown of St. Wenceslaus," imitating the Hungarian "sacred" symbol of the crown of St. Stephen. Some of them even expected a Bohemia from which the German "intruders" would be excluded, the ancestors of whom had settled in the Bohemian frontier lands many centuries ago upon the invitation of the Bohemian kings. The Bohemian Germans, on the other hand, were the most vigorous supporters of Pan-Germanism and racialism among the Austrians. Their leader Georg von Schönerer (1842-1921) wished to bring the Austrian Germans "home" into the German Empire, because he insisted that people of the same blood must be gathered in one state.

Among the Czechs an extreme radical party, calling itself National Socialists and composed mainly of the lower middle classes, was founded in 1898 under the leadership of Václav Klofáč (1868-1940). It openly espoused the cause of Pan-Slavism.

The antagonism among the Austrian nationalities even intruded into the officially supranational or international Austrian Social Democratic Party, which was founded in 1888 under the leadership of Dr. Viktor Adler (1852-1918). Accordingly the originally unified party was divided into national sections. Under the impact of this problem, leading Austrian Social Democrats like Dr. Karl Renner (1870-1950), who from 1945 to his death was the first president of the Second Austrian Republic as it emerged from World War II, and Dr. Otto Bauer (1882-1938) developed new theories of national autonomy, especially cultural autonomy, within a wider federal entity.

The Development among the Southern Slavs. The immediate cause of the catastrophe which overtook Austria-Hungary and the whole of Europe in 1914 was not the growing nationality conflict between Czechs and Germans but the growth of a south Slav *irredenta*. This word, meaning "unredeemed," was originally used by Italian nationalists for the Italian-speaking populations and their lands which were subject to non-Italian governments, and was later applied to similar situations elsewhere. An Italian *irredenta* existed also in the Habsburg Empire, though after the loss of Lombardy and Venetia the Italian-speaking population amounted to only about six hundred thousand, most of them concentrated in the Austrian seaport of Trieste and in the former bishopric of Trent in the southern tip of Tyrol. Outside Tyrol, the

Italians in the Habsburg Empire lived intermingled with southern Slavs—Slovenes and Croats—to whom they were numerically inferior, except in the cities, but economically and socially much superior. With the influx of peasant people to the cities and the growth of democracy the relation between the two peoples began to shift in favor of the southern Slavs. Thus it came about that Italian aspirations produced in the period of the First World War not only a conflict between Italy and the Habsburg Empire but also between Italy and the southern Slavs.

As the Italian *irredenta* was stimulated by the dynastic and military aspirations and pretensions of the Kingdom of Sardinia and its diplomatic successes, so the southern Slav *irredenta* was largely created and definitely intensified by the desire of the Kingdom of Serbia, which the Serbs living under Turkish domination carved in the course of the nineteenth century out of the Turkish Empire, to become the Sardinia of the southern Slavs. The southern Slav question was politically complicated by the fact that Serbs lived also in Hungary and in the formerly Turkish provinces of Bosnia-Herzegovina which were occupied by Austria-Hungary in 1878, and that the other southern Slav people, the Croats, lived partly in Austrian provinces and partly in the Kingdom of Croatia which was included in the lands of the Hungarian crown.

The small Serb principality which received autonomy from the Turkish overlords at the end of the Napoleonic Wars succeeded in the following decades not only in expanding territorially but in having its full sovereignty recognized in 1878 at the Congress of Berlin. Its prince, Milan Obrenović (ruled 1868-1889), assumed the title of king in 1882. He and his son Alexander (ruled 1889-1903) followed a pro-Austrian policy. The Obrenović and their policy were opposed by the Radical Party, which was founded in 1881 under the impact of the Populist Socialist Serb writer Svetozar Marković (1846-1875) who in spite of his early death became the most influential teacher and guide of Serbian youth. The leadership of the party was soon assumed by Nikola Pašić (1845-1926) who with a few interruptions dominated

Serbian policy from 1906 to his death. He was bent on aggrandizing Serbia not only at the expense of Turkey but also of Austria-Hungary and on establishing Serbian preponderance over the other southern Slav peoples, especially the Croats.

His opportunity came after the fall of the Obrenović dynasty, whose last representative, King Alexander, was assassinated in June 1903 by army officers. Among the plotters, Dragutin Dimitrijević, called "Apis," (1876-1917), played a leading role. This bloody end of princely rule was not an isolated episode in modern Serb history: of the nine princes who ruled Serbia between 1804 and 1941 no fewer than four were assassinated by their own people and four were dethroned. After Alexander's death, the sixty-year-old Peter I (ruled 1903-1921) of the family of the Karadgordgević was enthroned by the officers. His reign brought a new orientation of Serb policy. Peter had lived and served in France and he felt a strong tie to the Franco-Russian alliance. Pašić, who was a Russophile, became his foreign minister. A number of secret organizations, mostly composed of officers and students, of which "Union or Death," sometimes also called "The Black Hand," became the best known, began to agitate among the southern Slavs in the Turkish province of Macedonia and in the Habsburg Empire.

When Serbia refused in 1905 to renew its trade agreement with Austria-Hungary, the latter closed its frontiers to the importation of Serbian hogs, Serbia's chief export, of which Austria-Hungary until then had taken 83 per cent. This "hog war" which lasted for two years ended with a Serbian victory. With the help of French capital the Serbs were able to set up processing plants and to export their products through the port of Salonica to western Europe. In 1910 Austria-Hungary's part of the Serbian exports had fallen to 33 per cent. This episode considerably enhanced Serb self-confidence; two Serb victories in the First Balkan War (1912-1913) over Turkey, and in the Second Balkan War (1913) over Bulgaria, as a result of which Serbia acquired the long coveted province of Macedonia, seemed to make it a certainty for many Serbs that they were to become the liberators and the future overlords of the southern Slavs living under Habsburg domination.

This trend of unifying all the southern Slavs under Serbian Orthodox leadership was opposed by many Croats. Some of them envisaged a southern Slav union under Croat leadership within the Habsburg monarchy. The famous Catholic Bishop Josip Juraj Strossmayer (1815-1905) founded in 1867 the Yugoslav Academy in Zagreb, the Croatian capital, and in 1874 Zagreb became the seat of a university. Both institutions stimulated a Croatian cultural revival which looked for inspiration more to Vienna and the West than to Belgrade or Russia. Under the leadership of Ante Starčević (1823-1896) a Croatian Party of the Right was formed, the word "Right" implying, not a conservative or reactionary trend, but the insistence upon Croatian rights and upon their being right. This party envisaged the union of Croatia, Slovenia, and Dalmatia, sometimes regarding such a union as a starting point for southern Slav unity and stressing the cultural superiority of the Catholic Croats over the Orthodox Serbs. It hoped for the reconstruction of the Austro-Hungarian dual monarchy along trialist lines, giving the southern Slavs, united in a Greater Croatia, an equal status with Austria and Hungary. Archduke Francis Ferdinand was supposed to sympathize with this plan. Thus a Great Croatian idea faced the Great Serbian idea at the beginning of the twentieth century as a competitor for the solution of the southern Slav question. The ruling circles in Budapest tried to profit from Serb-Croatian antagonism. For twenty years (1883-1903) Count Charles Khuen-Héderváry (1849-1918) was *banus* or governor of Croatia and openly supported the Serb minority and the Orthodox religion against the Croats.

Whereas the party led by Starčević was composed above all of middle-class intelligentsia, a much more powerful peasant party took the lead at the beginning of the twentieth century. It was founded by Stjepan Radić (1871-1928). The party represented an agrarian socialism with federalist and pacifist features. But whether the southern Slavs were primarily Croat or Serb nationalists, they were all discontented with the *status quo* as established by the Compromise of 1867.

German and Italian Nationalism. Traditionally the Austrian Germans had been the most loyal supporters of the Habsburg monarchy. That remained on the whole true until the downfall of the monarchy in 1918. Pro-Habsburg sentiment even survived that downfall. But the exclusion of Austria from Germany in 1866 and the foundation of a new mighty German empire by Bismarck in 1871 created a feeling of dual loyalty among many Austrian Germans. This dual loyalty was in no way encouraged by the German government under Bismarck. On the contrary, Bismarck considered the preservation of a strong Habsburg monarchy to be in the interests of Germany and of European peace.

But with the growing influence of the Slavs in the monarchy a small section of the German population in Austria looked more and more across the frontiers to the rising star of Berlin and dreamt of union with the powerful imperial Germany. Thus they turned against the Habsburgs, whom they accused of a lack of German national feeling, and turned admiringly toward the Hohenzollern. The leader of this movement, which called itself Pan-German, was Georg von Schönerer (1842-1921). His opposition to the Habsburg monarchy inspired not only his violent hostility to the Slavs and Roman Catholicism but also to the Jews, whom he accused of dominating much of Austrian economic and cultural life. He developed a racial anti-Semitism which in many ways anticipated that of Adolf Hitler, who in his early years in Vienna came under Pan-German influence. Schönerer's party showed some strength in Bohemia, where the Germans were involved in a bitter struggle with the Czechs, and in Styria, where the Germans were involved in a similar struggle with the Slovenes. Many of Schönerer's adherents were found among university students and among high-school teachers, especially of history and of German.

The German lower middle class in Vienna and in many Alpine provinces was organized at the end of the nineteenth century by a Viennese lawyer, Karl Lueger (1844-

1910), who founded the Christian Social Party. Its program comprised fervent loyalty to the Catholic Church and to the Habsburg monarchy and equally fervent opposition to capitalism and to the Jews, who were regarded as a main bulwark of capitalism. Four times elected mayor of Vienna, Lueger was refused confirmation by Francis Joseph. Only on the occasion of his fifth election in 1897 was he confirmed and remained mayor of the Austrian capital until his death, carrying through many valuable reforms but strengthening through his demagogic oratory the anti-Semitic spirit, in that one respect working in the same direction as Schönerer with whom he otherwise disagreed in everything.

Whereas the Germans were one of the most numerous elements of the monarchy, the Italians formed only a small minority after Austria's loss of Lombardy and Venetia. They never were fervently loyal to the Habsburgs as many Germans were. Yet, like the Germans, they could look across the frontiers to the rise of a united Italian kingdom after 1861 and long for union with it. Under various forms many Italians kept up a ceaseless propaganda against Habsburg rule, especially in Trieste and in the Italian-speaking part of southern Tyrol. The Italian fanatics even resorted to terrorism. The best known case was that of a Triestine, William Oberdank, who planned to assassinate Francis Joseph and his wife when they visited Trieste in 1882 in celebration of the 500th anniversary of the attachment of the city to Austria. A bomb was thrown that killed and wounded several people. Oberdank, who confessed his intention of killing the monarch, was executed by the Austrian authorities but hailed in Italy as a glorious martyr. Anthems were written and monuments erected to his memory. Yet on other occasions the Italian population of the Habsburg monarchy showed its attachment to the dynasty. The Italian government, though probably not as sincerely as Bismarck, opposed the revolutionary agitation among the Austrian Italians and favored, at least until 1908, loyal cooperation with the Habsburg government.

Somewhat similar was the situation among the Rumanians in Transylvania. Whereas the Italians in Austria were in no way an oppressed minority and economically rather prosperous, the Rumanians in Hungary were an oppressed and poverty-stricken peasant population. They, too, began to look to the Kingdom of Rumania for support, and a League for the Cultural Unity of all Rumanians was founded at Bucharest, the kingdom's capital, in 1891 to promote Rumanian education and national feeling in the Rumanian parts of Hungary. Some Rumanians dreamt of a Greater Rumania, corresponding to the Greater Germany, the Greater Italy, or the Greater Serbia which at that period haunted excited minds in central Europe. But the Rumanian government on the whole followed, as did the Italian government, an attitude of correct restraint. All these developments among the nationalities of the monarchy complicated and aggravated its internal development and the growth of democracy.

— 6 —

DOMESTIC ISSUES FROM 1867 TO 1914

The Liberal Era. Amidst all the controversies and upheavals caused by the growing conflict of nationalities and by the vain search for an Austrian idea, the Austrian Constitution of December 31, 1867 (see above, p. 47), which was a document of mid-century liberalism, remained in force for over half a century. It was not changed except for a gradual broadening of the suffrage, which finally became for the last ten years of Austria's existence fully democratic, the vote being given to every male adult. The first Austrian government under the new constitution under Prince Carlos Auersperg (1814-1890), introduced a large measure of liberal reforms. Trial by jury was broadened to include judicial procedures connected with the freedom of the press. Elementary education was made free and compulsory throughout the realm. Preparations were made for the abrogation of the Concordat of 1855, according to which the Catholic Church had a preponderant influence in education and the exclusive jurisdiction over marriage and family law connected with it. The Concordat was abolished in 1871 and its abolition was helped by the fears aroused even in Catholic states by the new dogma of the infallibility of the pope.

The liberal ministry of Prince Auersperg devoted little attention, however, to the solution of the nationality problem. This problem became more acute after 1870, when the creation of the German Empire by Bismarck after defeat of France buried forever the hopes of the

Habsburgs to assume again a leading position in Germany. The Compromise with Hungary, to which the Slav people had been sacrificed, had been concluded primarily in the expectation of strengthening Austria for a possible resumption of the struggle with Prussia. Now the time seemed to have arrived for a compromise with the leading Slav nationality, the Czechs. In 1871 the attempt was made by the new cabinet presided over by Count Karl Siegmund Hohenwart (1824-1899), a conservative and clerical aristocrat. The outstanding man of the ministry was Albert Schäffle (1831-1900), an economist from Württemberg in southwestern Germany who in 1868 became professor at the University of Vienna. A liberal and a federalist, he wished to reorganize the Empire on a federal basis, introducing at the same time universal suffrage and broad social reform. The cabinet, which counted among its members two Czechs and one Pole, entered into negotiations with Czech leaders, above all with Dr. Rieger, about a federal solution which would have given the German and Czech languages equal official status in Bohemia. Francis Joseph declared his readiness not only to recognize the rights of the Bohemian kingdom but to confirm this assurance by being crowned at Prague with the ancient crown of St. Wenceslaus and by taking the coronation oath. This coronation in Prague would have paralleled the coronation in Budapest in 1867. But the resistance of the Germans and above all of the Magyars wrecked this compromise. (*See Reading No. 12.*)

The Hohenwart ministry resigned. Schäffle returned to his native Württemberg. The Magyar position in the Empire was strengthened by the Hungarian Prime Minister Julius Andrássy assuming the office of foreign minister for the dual monarchy. In Austria itself a ministry was formed under Prince Adolf Auersperg (1821-1885), a brother of Carlos Auersperg. He himself was a strict constitutionalist, fair and impartial. Under him the electoral law was reformed. The members of the Reichsrat, the Imperial Council or Parliament, were no longer delegated by the provincial diets but chosen in direct elections. The number of seats was substantially increased. The representatives were chosen according to four curiae or socio-economic electoral bodies: great landed proprietors, the urban middle class, the chambers of commerce, and finally the rural communes. The right to vote in the latter three groups was tied to property qualifications.

The Czech deputies boycotted the parliamentary sessions. Nevertheless, the parliament dominated by the German liberals carried in the first years some prestige thanks to the progressive industrialization of the country. The building of new railroads was actively promoted and the World Fair in Vienna in 1873 promised to be a great success. But in the same year, as a result of over-speculation, an economic depression hit the country and a number of cases of corruption, in which members of parliament were involved, were revealed. The opposition of many German liberals to Austria-Hungary's foreign policy in the Balkans brought the fall of the cabinet in February 1879.

The Breathing Spell. Francis Joseph turned now to Count Edward Taaffe (1833-1895), a conservative aristocrat who enjoyed his full confidence. He did not belong to any party nor to any nationality and regarded himself as a representative of the interests of the empire as a whole. "I shall never leave the constitutional basis," he declared on taking office, "if only because the Emperor stands on this basis and is the firmest supporter of the Constitution, a true, genuinely constitutional monarch." For fourteen years he succeeded in governing Austria without any major opposition. He described his policy as "keeping all the nationalities in a balanced state of mild dissatisfaction" and during his reign of stability Austria seemed farther away from the collapse which many had feared during the preceding thirty years.

The Czech deputies returned to participation in parliamentary life. The Czech language was given equality with German in education and in the administrative contacts of the citizens with the government. A growing number of civil servants from among the Czechs and the other non-German nationalities were appointed. In

1882 the right to vote in the cities and in the rural district was given to all citizens who paid five florins ($2.50) in direct taxes.

In spite of some bitter complaints voiced by the Czechs, they made great economic and cultural progress during the time. A well-educated Czech middle class grew rapidly and took commanding positions in economic and political life. In 1868 Emil Škoda (1839-1900) acquired a machine plant which had been established in Pilsen (Plzeň) in 1859 and built it up into the most important and best equipped armament works in the Austro-Hungarian monarchy. In the same year the first large Czech bank was founded to promote Czech industrial and commercial development. In the 1880's, which saw also the establishment of a representative Czech National Theater and of a Czech university, Bohemia had become economically and industrially the most advanced province of the dual monarchy.

In 1890 Taaffe undertook a new attempt to solve the nationality problem by dividing the provinces in which two or several nationalities lived and more than one language was spoken into administrative districts according to ethnic and linguistic lines. The more conservative Czechs and Germans were willing to cooperate, but in Bohemia the Old Czechs who followed Rieger were pushed into the background by the more radical Young Czechs, and a similar process of radicalization had gone on among the Germans. In the elections of 1891 the Young Czechs won a victory, electing 37 deputies as against 12 Old Czechs. In that situation Taaffe sought to appeal to the masses, the peasants and even the workers, by the introduction of universal suffrage. He hoped that they would prefer economic reforms to nationalist demands. But the opposition of the privileged parties and nationalities was too strong. Taaffe resigned in 1893. Short-lived coalition ministries took over. Parliamentary life was now wrecked by bitter nationality conflicts over what appeared objectively trifling matters. (*See Reading No. 13.*) The demand for general suffrage, once officially raised, could not be avoided for long. The

Social Democratic Party took it up and organized, for the first time, impressive and orderly workers' demonstrations in the streets.

The Crisis of 1897. In 1895 the Emperor turned to the Polish aristocrat, Count Kasimir Badeni (1846-1909) who enjoyed a reputation as a strong man. He carried through a moderate suffrage reform by establishing a fifth curia in which every male citizen over 24 received the right to vote. The elections held in March 1897 on the basis of the new franchise brought the definitive victory of the Young Czechs in Bohemia over the Old Czechs. Badeni could find a majority only by securing the cooperation of the Czechs. For that purpose he promulgated a new language ordinance in April 1897, according to which Czech and German would have equal rights in the administrative services in all parts of Bohemia. For practical purposes it meant that all civil servants in Bohemia and Moravia would have to possess a speaking and writing knowledge of both languages. Such a provision practically favored the Czechs, who learned German in school, whereas the Germans had refused to learn the "inferior" language of their Czech fellow citizens.

The language ordinance led to bitter demonstrations on the part of the Germans both in parliament and in the streets. For a short while the disorders threatened to grow into a revolution. Intemperate language was used on all sides, the bitterness grew, university students and youth took a leading part in noisy demonstrations, and even after Badeni's resignation the days of the relative calm prevailing under Taaffe never returned.

Austria entered now the last and critical stage of its existence. The Emperor had grown old. In 1898 he celebrated the fiftieth anniversary of his accession to the throne, and on the same day martial law had to be proclaimed in Prague, to contain violent Czech demonstrations connected with the repeal of Badeni's language ordinances. But the Emperor aroused among all the people feelings of personal sympathy and loyalty, partly due to the tragedies of his private life—the suicide of his only son in 1889 and the assassination in Geneva of his

wife Elizabeth, a Bavarian princess famed for her beauty
and grace, by an Italian anarchist in 1898. The Emperor
was a lonely old man defending what seemed to many a
forlorn post. It was often said that the monarchy was
tied up with his life and might not survive him. He was
its living symbol and yet seemed a survivor of a past age.

In 1900, when Austria entered the new century—a
century of unprecedented upheavals and violence—the
monarch was seventy years old. The domestic difficulties
were intensified by two new elements, the growing
turbulence of an extreme Magyar nationalism which
threatened to undermine the Compromise of 1867, and
a sequence of crises in foreign policy, growing in rapidity
and intensity, in all of which Austria and her chief ally,
the German Empire created by Bismarck in 1871, were
centrally involved.

Crisis in Hungary. In 1890 Kálmán Tisza resigned as prime minister of Hungary (see above, page
59). This resignation coincided with a change in the
public temper of the country. The older generation had
recognized the necessity of a strong great-power position
for the Dual Monarchy in the interests of Hungary itself.
The younger generation which now came to the fore, in
a spirit of exaggerated nationalism and overconfidence
believed in the strength of Hungary to stand alone and
even to expand its imperial mission over subject nationalities.

The leader of this new generation was first Count
Albert Apponyi (1846-1933), a brilliant orator who
recognized the influence of nationalist slogans upon the
masses. Beginning in 1878 he was a leader of the opposition in the Hungarian parliament, and in 1919 he
was the head of the Hungarian delegation to the Paris
Peace Conference. National self-confidence was nurtured
by the great progress achieved in Hungary since the
Compromise. The two cities of Buda and Pest were
transformed after their union in 1873 into a representative modern capital, in which the new parliament building
occupied a leading place. There had been growth in industry and railroads. The fame of the most widely read
Hungarian novelist, Mór Jókai (1825-1904) spread

throughout Europe. János Arany (1817-1882) was the greatest Hungarian epic poet. Later and more modern writers were Endre Ady (1877-1919) who was influenced by contemporary French literature, and Mihály Babits (1883-1941). A national school of composers, based upon Hungarian folk music, grew up in Béla Bartók (1881-1945) and his friend Zoltán Kodály (b. 1882) and represented an important contribution to the development of modern music.

Nationalist sentiment was spurred even more by large public celebrations. In 1894 the aged Kossuth died in exile and was buried in Hungary. His son Ferenc became the leader of the extreme Independence Party. Two years later the thousandth anniversary of the Magyar invasion and conquest of Hungary was celebrated and a millennial fair was held. In 1898 similarly, the fiftieth anniversary of the revolution of 1848 aroused the enthusiasm of Magyar nationalism, and the year 1902 witnessed the celebration of the centennial of Kossuth's birth. The rising demand for ending the Compromise of 1867 and for establishing Hungary's complete independence has to be seen against this background. This demand centered around two problems: the creation of an independent Hungarian army with the Magyar language as the language of command and with the Hungarian flag of red, white, and green as its standard, and the establishment of Hungarian economic independence by ending the customs and monetary union with Austria. In spite of the fact that three-fourths of Hungarian agricultural products, the main export of the country, were taken by Austria, a boycott of Austrian industrial products was proclaimed.

The ruling oligarchy overlooked the fact that its nationalist policy was in no way national. It expressed the desire of a small ruling group. It was not supported by the national minorities who formed more than half of the population nor by the Magyar masses themselves, who were more interested in land reform and in combatting the socially and economic backward conditions which prevailed in many parts of the country. Their opposition was, of course, of little avail. More important was that of Francis Joseph, who resisted the attempt to undermine the great-power position of the monarchy, which he believed of vital importance for Hungary, too.

Francis Joseph made his resolution of maintaining the unity of the Austro-Hungarian army known in an army order issued at the end of the maneuvers in September 1903, at which he was present, at Chlopy in Galicia. He emphasized that the army must be guided by the spirit of unity and harmony which would respect and honor every national individuality and would use the advantages of each people to the benefit of the whole. In this critical situation Tisza's son István (Stephen) became prime minister. The Crown made various concessions in the army question; on the other hand, Tisza maintained "for weighty political reasons affecting great interests of the nation . . . the standpoint that the king has a right to fix the language of service and command in the Hungarian army."

The bill proposed by Tisza was enacted into law, but the disorders of the noisy opposition grew to such an extent that he dissolved the Chamber. In the elections at the beginning of 1905 Tisza was defeated. Francis Joseph appointed a nonparliamentary cabinet which threatened to submit the dispute between the Crown and the extreme Magyar nationalists to the test of universal suffrage. But a democratization of the franchise in Hungary would have ended the entrenched supremacy of the Magyars over the other nationalities and that of the Magyar nobility and gentry over the poorer classes. This fact and also the mounting economic crisis in Hungary brought the opposition around to accepting economic cooperation with Austria, though under terms unduly favoring Magyar separatism. Yet it was reasonably clear that an independent Hungarian tariff system and the establishment of an independent Hungarian national bank instead of the common Austro-Hungarian national bank would have had grave consequences for Hungarian economy and finances. Such considerations, however, weighed little with the Magyar nationalists. Their opposition to the Crown coincided with a hardening of their domineering attitude towards the non-Magyar nationalities (*see*

Reading No. 14) and especially towards the southern
Slavs. By this latter attitude they broadened the gulf between Magyars and Croats and drove the latter into the
arms of the Serbs. By the weakening of the international
position of the monarchy and by the policy towards
their own minorities, the Magyar nationalists helped to
prepare the catastrophe which in 1918 engulfed not only
the monarchy but the long and deeply cherished Magyar
supremacy.

In 1913 Tisza became again prime minister of Hungary. He succeeded in imposing his iron will upon the
opposition. No serious effort, however, was made to
bring about the much needed social reforms and an
amelioration in the situation of the minorities. The public
opinion of the Magyar ruling class remained fascinated
by an illusion-fraught policy of independence, thus contributing to the incipient disintegration of the monarchy.
Sterile constitutional questions took precedence over the
preservation of a large economic unit which would
promote the development of industry and secure a rising
standard of living.

This problem was understood not in Hungary but in
Austria, especially among the Social Democrats, who
rapidly grew in numbers. But at the same time the
Austrian half of the Habsburg Empire suffered in
power and prestige from the chaotic conditions which
prevailed, as a result of the nationality struggle, in its
parliament, and from the weakness of the cabinets which
followed each other with great rapidity. Compared with
Austria, Hungary gave the impression of a consolidated
political entity, owing to its ancient parliamentary structure upheld by antiquated and corrupt elections and to
a semicolonial regime maintained in the non-Magyar
parts of the kingdom. In Austria there was much discussion among a few far-sighted theoreticians of the
need of a federal transformation of the Dual Monarchy,
including its Hungarian part, but there was neither the
practical experience of orderly parliamentary life nor
the will to establish a lasting compromise which would
make such a life and the reorganization of the monarchy
possible.

Crisis in Permanence. Yet this period of permanent political crisis was at the same time like a glowing sunset for the Habsburg monarchy in other fields. Austria reached an unprecedented position in its cultural life and economic and social progress was rapid. More than ever before Vienna became a center of European music and scholarship and of new German writing. It was a truly imperial and cosmopolitan city. From end to end of the realm young talents gathered there. The University School of Medicine was world famous and attracted especially many students from the United States. Almost equally important was the School of Law, with Rudolf von Jhering (1818-1892), the founder of the modern philosophico-historical school of law, and Joseph Unger (1828-1913). In opposition to the prevailing German historical school of political economy, the Viennese economists, of whom Karl Menger (1840-1921) was the best known, developed a new and theoretical approach to the problems of economy. Sigmund Freud (1856-1939) opened in 1900, with his *The Interpretation of Dreams* a new era of the treatment and of the interpretation of neurosis and other psychic phenomena.

At the same time Vienna revived as the foremost center of musical life in Europe. Among the older generation were Anton Bruckner (1824-1896) and Johannes Brahms (1833-1897) who, born in Hamburg, lived in Vienna after 1862. Hugo Wolf (1860-1903) became famous as a composer of *lieder*. The modern school of musical composition started in Vienna with Gustav Mahler (1860-1911) and his two disciples Arnold Schönberg (1874-1951) and Alban Berg (1885-1935). Mahler was also musical director of the Viennese Court Opera House, which became the leading operatic stage in Europe.

A similar rank in the dramatic arts was held by the Hofburgtheater, which moved into its new magnificent building in 1888. The Viennese public has been for a long time more theater-minded than that of any other metropolitan city. Events in the theater played a great role in the daily life of the citizens and were widely discussed in all circles. Great actors like Adolf von Sonnenthal

(1834-1909), who joined the Burgtheater in 1856, and Josef Kainz (1858-1910), who joined it in 1899, were among Vienna's most popular figures. Of the many gifted writers who also wrote for the theater, only Arthur Schnitzler (1862-1931), Karl Schönherr (1867-1943), and the poet Hugo von Hofmannsthal (1874-1929) can be mentioned here.

One field of musical and theatrical production spread its influence far abroad as a characteristically Viennese contribution—the operetta, and with it the waltz. Johann Strauss (1825-1899), the son of the older Johann Strauss (1804-1849), contributed with his father and brothers most of the fame of the Viennese waltz and of the reputed gaiety of the imperial city. In his "The Blue Danube" he probably wrote the best of all waltzes. He wrote also many operettas or light operas. *Die Fledermaus* (1874) still holds its place on the great opera stages of the world. Hardly less popular was *The Merry Widow* (1905) by Franz Lehár (1870-1948), who, born in Hungary, lived in Austria and was from 1890 to 1902 bandmaster of various Austrian regiments.

But this gaiety was in contrast to the darkening political clouds on the horizon, which gathered strength with the beginning of the twentieth century. In 1900 Francis Joseph appointed Dr. Ernest Koerber (1850-1919) prime minister, a position which he filled until December 1904. A highly able administrator, he introduced a number of economic projects and reforms, hoping thereby to overcome nationality conflicts in a common feeling of progress and prosperity. But very soon it was difficult to find a coherent majority in the Reichstag. Under these conditions Koerber and the following cabinets had recourse to Article 14 of the constitutional law of 1867. This empowered the government to issue "emergency regulations" in case of need which would remain valid unless repudiated by the Reichsrat. National peace could not be established in Bohemia, which remained the most embattled field of conflict between Germans and Czechs. But soon afterwards, in the province of Moravia, Bohemia's neighbor, inhabited by both Czechs and Germans, and in the province of Bucovina, east of Galicia, where three nationalities—Ukrainian, Rumanian and German—lived together, it was possible to establish an agreed-upon compromise which allowed the provincial diets to work normally and peacefully and which brought about a settlement satisfactory to all the nationalities involved.

In this situation the Crown took the initiative in proposing the introduction of general direct and universal suffrage in Austria. (*See Reading No. 15.*) Francis Joseph naturally was not guided in this step by any democratic ideology. The old parliament had shown itself unworkable. By giving the vote to the masses there was hope that they prove less nationalistic than their middle-class leaders and that they might cooperate in a program of social progress and economic development for all the nationalities. The situation in Hungary and the Russian Revolution of 1905 provided other incentives for the introduction of democracy. Under the pressure of the Crown the parliament accepted the electoral reform on December 1, 1906, and it became law on January 26, 1907. The new democratic parliament was opened on June 17, 1907.

The new parliament counted 516 members. The strongest single party was the Social Democrats, who received 87 seats. Of the deputies, 254 were Slavs, 231 were Germans, 19 were Italians, and there were in addition 6 Rumanians and 5 Jewish nationalists. But all the larger nationality groups were split into many parties. It should not be overlooked that Austria now possessed a democratic parliament but no democratic administration. The constitution did not foresee a parliamentary regime with a cabinet representing the parliamentary majority and responsible to parliament. The ministers were appointed by the Crown and were responsible to it. In the large majority they were not parliamentarians but civil servants. They tried to find shifting working majorities from among the parties represented in the parliament to carry through various pieces of legislation. Perhaps if there had been time given and if the Magyar oligarchy could have been curbed, the introduction of democracy might have saved the Austro-Hungarian monarchy.

The English historian A. J. P. Taylor, no friend of the monarchy, remarked that by 1914 in every Austrian province "except Bohemia the peoples had found or were finding local solutions; and every nationality in Austria, except the Italians and a [small] minority of the Germans, preferred the Habsburg monarchy to any [then] conceivable alternative. . . ." But even in Bohemia "the Czechs and Germans were fighting each other in order to extract concessions from the monarchy. No party on either side seriously desired the break-up of Austria-Hungary." This situation changed only when the monarchy was drawn into the maelstrom of European power politics which its own domestic tensions and its own foreign policy helped to aggravate.

7

FOREIGN POLICY 1871 TO 1914

The Alliance with Germany. The events of 1870-1871 marked a turning point in European history. Under Bismarck's leadership Prussia defeated France, united the German states under Prussian leadership and established this new German Empire as the foremost power in Europe. These events left a legacy of great bitterness with the French, who until then had been favorably inclined toward Prussia. The growing aspirations of the new German Empire in the following decades alienated first Russia, which had been for 150 years on the whole a friend and ally of Prussia, and finally Britain, which throughout the nineteenth century had regarded Russia and France, not Germany, as the main threat to her position. Under these circumstances Bismarck's Germany found its only reliable friend in the Habsburg monarchy, a rather strange fact if one takes into consideration that Bismarck erected his empire on the forcible ejection of Habsburg influence from Germany and Italy.

After 1866 Francis Joseph hoped to undo this ejection. This hope came to a definite end with Bismarck's victory in 1871. The whole trend of Habsburg policy changed, away from aspirations of playing a role in Germany to the possibility of growing influence in the Balkans. The place of Beust as foreign minister, whose interest centered upon Germany and who was a bitter adversary of Bismarck, was now taken by the Magyar aristocrat Gyula Andrássy. He was a fervent admirer of Bismarck and of his Germany. As a Magyar, he distrusted Russian ex-

pansion and agreed with Britain about the need for pre-
serving the Ottoman Empire. He saw the future of the
monarchy in the economic penetration of the Balkans
and promoted the construction of a railroad linking
Vienna and Budapest with Constantinople and the Aegean
port of Salonica, then a part of Turkey, today belonging to Greece.

The pattern of the future was prefigured by visits
which Francis Joseph paid to his fellow monarchs. The
nineteenth century was a period in which monarchs and
dynastic relations still determined foreign policy. Thus
meetings of monarchs were indicative of general trends.
In 1872 the German Emperor William I, the Russian
Emperor Alexander II, and Francis Joseph met in Berlin.
The meeting of the three eastern monarchs restored to a
certain extent the Holy Alliance formed by their predecessors in 1815, which had been in the same way devoted
to the defense of conservative and monarchical interests
in Europe. The meeting between the Russian and the
Austrian Emperors went far toward liquidating the bitterness caused by Austria's attitude in the Crimean War.
In 1873 King Victor Emmanuel II of Italy visited Francis
Joseph in Vienna, eager to improve relations with Austria
in order that the latter might not support papal claims
to the restoration of the Roman territory annexed in
1870 by the Italian kingdom. In 1874 Francis Joseph
paid a state visit to St. Petersburg and in the following
year met the Italian king in Venice, which less than
ten years before had been Austrian. As a faithful
Catholic he could not pay an official visit to the King
of Italy in Rome because such a step would have aroused
the bitter ire of Pope Pius IX, who never forgot or for-
gave the spoliation of his temporal power by Victor
Emmanuel.

As a result of the Balkan crisis which started in 1875
and which will be discussed in the next section, Bismarck
and Andrássy concluded a dual alliance between Austria-
Hungary and Germany which was ratified on October 17,
1879. It was a defensive alliance directed against Russia,
originally a secret treaty to run for five years but renewed
in various forms so that it lasted until the end of the

Habsburg monarchy and formed the backbone of its
foreign policy. This treaty and the foreign policy which
it indicated were welcomed by the Magyars and by the
Austrian-Germans. For most of the time the Austrian
Poles in their dislike of Russia supported it too. But
it alienated most of the Austrian Slavs, above all the
Czechs, who feared German and Magyar much more
than Russian expansion and who felt a cultural sympathy
for the French. After the conclusion of the treaty with
Germany, Andrássy, who regarded it as his handiwork,
withdrew from the foreign office.

The Balkan Crisis. Andrássy found the emperor's
backing for the alliance with Bismarck's Germany because in the preceding years Austria had felt herself
threatened by Russian moves in the Balkans. The pretext
for Russia's intervention in the Balkans was provided by
an uprising of the Slav Christian subjects of the Ottoman Sultan in two Turkish provinces—in Bosnia-Herzegovina which bordered on Austria, and in Bulgaria. The
Bulgarian uprising led to a Russian Turkish War. This
started in 1877 and ended the following February with
a peace treaty which established a Greater Bulgaria,
regarded by Britain and by Austria as a Russian satellite.
Its creation threatened to destroy completely the Turkish
position in Europe and the equilibrium of the forces in
the Balkans. As a result the European powers insisted
on the convocation of a European Congress in Berlin
in the summer of 1878 to settle the Balkan problems.
Andrássy assured himself of British support for his plans
of occupying the two Turkish provinces of Bosnia-Herzegovina, which would nominally remain part of the
Turkish Empire but would be put under Austrian administration, a situation similar to that created in Cyprus
in 1878 and in Egypt in 1882 in favor of Britain. Though
there was no unanimous domestic backing for Andrássy's
plans—many Germans and Magyars resented the addition of further Slavs to the monarchy—he succeeded
at Berlin in receiving a European mandate for the occupation of the two Turkish provinces. He also secured
special privileges in an adjoining third Turkish province,
that of Novibazar, which stretches from the southern

end of Bosnia in a southeasterly direction, separating
Serbia from Montenegro and opening up a corridor to
Salonica.

The Austrian occupation forces ran into difficulties
when they marched into Bosnia. The population of the
two provinces was divided among Roman Catholic, Greek
Orthodox, and Mohammedan populations. Only the
Roman Catholics, who felt themselves as Croatians,
welcomed the Austro-Hungarian troops. The Orthodox
population, regarding itself as Serbian, desired union
with Serbia, and the Mohammedans wished to remain
part of Turkey. It was the Serbian part of the population
which kept alive the bitter memory of the resistance
after it was crushed in 1879. This memory became the
seed of future Serbian fanaticism.

With Turkey, Austria-Hungary arrived at an agreement in April 1879 about Turkish residual rights and
privileges in the occupied provinces. Their administration
was entrusted to an Austro-Hungarian governor under
the supervision of the Austro-Hungarian minister of
common finances. The work of modernization of the
country began.

But the occupation of Bosnia-Herzegovina had far-
reaching and on the whole unfavorable consequences for
the Habsburg monarchy. It alienated not only the Russians and the Serbians but also the Italians, who regarded
at least the western Balkans as their own sphere of imperial expansion and were bitterly jealous of any growth
of Austrian influence there. A new birth of Italian aggressive nationalism found a vent in violent anti-Austrian
demonstrations and in outcries for the redemption of
Italia irredenta. This, according to the Italians, included
the Austrian province of Dalmatia, inhabited almost
wholly by southern Slavs of which Bosnia-Herzegovina
formed the hinterland. This situation drove Austria-
Hungary into the alliance with Germany and was one
of the factors contributing to the crises of the early
twentieth century in which the monarchy was to perish.

The Triple Alliance. In spite of the tensions created by the occupation of Bosnia-Herzegovina and
Andrássy's forward policy in the Balkans, Austria-Hun-

gary preserved for the following quarter of a century relations that were on the whole friendly with all her neighbors. Andrássy retired at the end of 1879, and after a brief interlude he was followed by Count Gustav Siegmund Kálnoky (1832-1898), a Moravian nobleman, and Count Agenor Goluchowski the Younger (1849-1921), a Polish conservative. These two men directed the foreign policy of the dual monarchy for twenty-five years, Kálnoky from 1881 to 1895 and Goluchowski from 1895 to 1906. Both were concerned with maintaining good relations with Russia. This task was facilitated by the fact that Russia's imperial ambitions were absorbed from 1890 to 1905 in the Far East. But already before that period, in 1881, the League of the Three Emperors settled for three years outstanding Balkan problems to the satisfaction of Germany, Russia, and Austria-Hungary, and the treaty was renewed in 1884 for three more years.

Of more lasting importance, though in the end also futile, was the Triple Alliance between Austria-Hungary, Germany, and Italy, concluded on May 20, 1882, and still in force, though in somewhat changed form, when the War of 1914 broke out. Bismarck agreed to include Italy in his system of alliances "to protect the Italian monarchy from the dangers which must inevitably arise from an alliance by treaty with France and from the reciprocal support of the radical elements of France and Italy." King Umberto of Italy visited Vienna in 1881. At that time Italy found herself thwarted in her imperial ambitions in North Africa by French occupation of Tunisia. The Italian dynasty felt itself threatened by papal and clerical opposition on the one side and republican sentiment on the other. In an alliance with powerful monarchist Germany, Italy hoped to find support for the crown and a stronger position in the Mediterranean against France. As Bismarck insisted on the inclusion of Austria-Hungary, the Italians had to abandon, at least officially, their claims to Italian-speaking parts of Austria. But the alliance between Italy and Austria-Hungary never became popular in either of the two countries.

The Triple Alliance reëstablished in the center of Europe a unity of policy which had existed after 1815, then under Habsburg leadership. Now the leadership had shifted to Berlin. The Triple Alliance also prefigured the Central European axis established in 1938, again linking the three capitals of Berlin, Vienna, and Rome. This time there was an even more marked preponderance of Berlin, which had by then pushed Vienna into an entirely subordinate position. The Triple Alliance, which lasted for over thirty years, brought in the long run no blessing to Europe or to Austria-Hungary. Bismarck, who tried to keep Russia friendly, succeeded in replacing the League of the Three Emperors in 1887 with a tortuous reassurance treaty which, however, was allowed to lapse in 1890 when Bismarck was removed from leadership in Germany.

In the 1880's the relations of the dual monarchy with Serbia and Rumania were good, but these good relations were backed in the two countries by the rulers and the courts, not by popular sentiment or the nationalist leadership. More cordial were Austro-Hungarian relations with Britain and France. In 1887 the Habsburg monarchy entered into a Mediterranean agreement with Britain and Italy which lasted until 1895. No cause or reason existed to create any tension between the Habsburg monarchy and the Western powers. Austria-Hungary had no colonial empire or ambitions and her navy was confined to the Adriatic Sea. French statesmen regarded the existence of the Habsburg monarchy as a necessary counterweight to German expansion and as an essential element in the preservation of the balance of power in Europe.

The Triple Alliance changed the whole picture. After Bismarck's dismissal, it led to the formation of an opposite dual alliance between Russia and France. These two powers were twenty years later joined in a loose but unmistakable Entente by Britain. Thus Austria-Hungary as Germany's partner was drawn into a European power struggle which was of no immediate concern to the Habsburg monarchy. As a result, a conflict between Austria-Hungary and one of its neighbors could not remain localized but threatened to bring about a general European war. Such a war, whatever its outcome, might destroy the European state system which since the settlement of Vienna in 1815 had maintained a sometimes precarious European stability. Thus the Triple Alliance carried in itself the seed of a grave threat to the future of Austria-Hungary and of Europe.

In his *Reflections and Reminiscences* published after his death in 1898, Prince Bismarck discussed the reasons which induced him to conclude the alliance with the Habsburg monarchy. As he wrote himself, after the victory over France and the annexation of Alsace-Lorraine, the idea of an anti-German coalition gave him nightmares. He was above all afraid of a re-creation of the coalition of France, Austria, and Russia, which the Austrian chancellor Count Wenzel Anton von Kaunitz (1711-1794) succeeded in cementing for the Seven Years' War against Prussia and which until Russia withdrew from the alliance put the Prussia of Frederick the Great into mortal danger. "This situation," Bismarck writes, "demanded an effort to limit the range of the possible anti-German coalition by means of treaty arrangements placing our relations with at least one of the Great Powers upon a firm footing. The choice could only lie between Austria and Russia. . . . In point of material force I held a union with Russia to have the advantage. I had also been used to regard it as safer, because I placed more reliance on traditional dynastic friendship, on community of conservative monarchical instincts, on the absence of indigenous political divisions, than on the fits and starts of public opinion among the Hungarian, Slav and Catholic population of the monarchy of the Habsburgs." (*See Reading No. 16.*)

When finally Bismarck gave the preference to the alliance with Austria, he was not blind to the perplexities which made a choice difficult. Yet he was determined to maintain good relations between Germany and Russia, because "our principal concern is to keep the peace between our two imperial neighbors. We shall be able to assure the future of the fourth great dynasty in Italy in proportion as we succeed in maintaining the unity of the three [eastern] empire states, and in either bridling the ambition of our two neighbors on the east or satisfying it by an *entente cordiale* with both. Both are for us indispensable elements in the European political equilibrium; the lack of either would be our peril—but the maintenance of monarchical government in Vienna and St. Petersburg . . . is for us in Germany a problem which coincides with the maintenance of our own state regime." After Bismarck's dismissal the *entente cordiale* with Russia was abandoned. The results were foreseen by Bismarck—a European war and the collapse of the three dynasties. The road to this war and to the collapse of the monarchical regimes led through the second Balkan crisis.

The Second Balkan Crisis. In 1906 new foreign secretaries were appointed in Russia and in Austria-Hungary. The former was Alexander Izvolsky (1856-1919), who had been Russian envoy to Japan and who regarded as his first task the liquidation of Russia's Far Eastern ventures and then the consolidation of Russia's ties with France and her *rapprochement* with Britain. He was instrumental in 1907 in settling the outstanding controversies between Britain and Russia. The new Austrian foreign secretary was Alois Lexa von Aehrenthal (1854-1912), who prior to his appointment had been for seven years Austrian ambassador in St. Petersburg. With him a new, active Austrian foreign policy began. Its purpose was to strengthen the prestige of the monarchy by the annexation of Bosnia-Herzegovina, the Turkish provinces which under Austrian administration had made great progress. (*See Reading No. 17.*)

The Balkan crisis started with the seizure of power in the Ottoman Empire by a group of officers, the Young Turks, who intended to introduce a modernizing and constitutional regime in the ancient and ramshackle empire. Austria-Hungary was sympathetic to a strengthening of Turkey, but other countries, above all the Christian Balkan nations, feared it as upsetting their plan for expansion at Turkey's expense. Even before the Young Turk revolution, Aehrenthal had discussed unofficially with Izvolsky his intention to annex Bosnia and Herzegovina and to build a railroad in the direction of Salonica. Izvolsky on his part desired to obtain for Russia the freedom of navigation in the Straits of Constantinople. After the Young Turk revolution, in September 1908, the two statesmen met at Buchlau, the Moravian residence of Count Leopold Berchtold (1863-1942), then the Austrian ambassador to St. Petersburg and later in 1912 Aehrenthal's successor as foreign secretary.

It never clearly transpired what the agreement reached at Buchlau was. Izvolsky certainly agreed to the annexation of Bosnia-Herzegovina, but he apparently demanded that it be referred to a European conference which would also decide on the freedom of the Straits for Russia. Aehrenthal did not understand it this way and apparently acted in good faith when he announced the annexation on October 5, 1908. (*See Reading No. 18.*) Izvolsky felt himself deceived because Britain and France refused to open the Straits question at that moment. The mutual hostility and distrust between the two statesmen which ensued paralleled the growing hostility between their two states. Izvolsky sought compensation for what he regarded as his diplomatic defeat in a meeting between the Emperor of Russia and the King of Italy in October 1909. This meeting was the first serious effort to draw Italy away from the Triple Alliance, after Italy had first arrived at a tentative *rapprochement* with France in 1902.

Aehrenthal hoped to make it clear to the world that the annexation was not the beginning of an expansionist policy on the part of the Dual Monarchy in the Balkans. To that end he renounced the project of the Balkan railroad and withdrew the Austrian garrisons from the Turkish province of Novibazar, where they had been stationed since 1878. But his principal mistake was in not taking into account the general tense atmosphere in Europe and the inevitable suspicions which any active step in the Balkans would arouse. It was the common fault, shared by the Austro-Hungarian and the German foreign offices before World War I, of lacking understanding of the psychological effects of their actions. They had not enough imagination to foresee the entirely foreseeable reactions of other nations. In the case of Germany the reason for this attitude was arrogant self-confidence; in

the case of Aehrenthal and Berchtold it was an aristocratic disregard for public opinion.

At first the Austrian Slav deputies, including the
Czechs and the southern Slavs, supported Aehrenthal's
policy and voted in the Austro-Hungarian delegation in
an overwhelming majority for the annexation. They saw
in it a potential strengthening of the Slav element in the
Habsburg monarchy. Especially the Croats welcomed the
measure which promised to make Croatia and not Serbia
the center of Yugoslav unity. But the Austro-Hungarian
government missed the opportunity for a positive southern
Slav policy and this failure brought Croats and Serbs
together. Outside the monarchy the annexation of Bosnia-
Herzegovina estranged Russia and Italy and aroused
strong hostility among the Serbs. Only with the Turks
could Aehrenthal arrive at an agreement in 1909 recog-
nizing the annexation.

Serbia even seemed ready to go to war against Austria-
Hungary, but Russia, weakened by the war against Japan
and by the Revolution of 1905 and warned by Germany,
refused to support Serbia and so the war was averted.
On the other hand there was in Austria-Hungary a small
group led by Franz Count Conrad von Hötzendorf (1852-
1925) who had become in 1906 chief of the general
staff, which wished to start a preventive war against
Serbia and above all, against Italy. Conrad von Hötzendorf was convinced that war was inevitable if Austria-
Hungary wished to preserve its position as a great power
or even perhaps its existence. He believed that such a
war could be easily won in 1908 and that with every
succeeding year the situation would become more unfavorable for the Dual Monarchy. Yet Aehrenthal opposed this policy and even forced in 1911 the resignation
of the chief of staff, who, however, was reappointed in
1912, being without doubt the most capable and perhaps
the only capable high officer in the army. Above all
Emperor Francis Joseph, who in spite of his advanced
age remained the central figure in the Empire, was dead
set against any war and wished to preserve, certainly for
the remainder of his life, the *status quo*. (*See Reading
No. 19.*)

But the *status quo* in the Balkans did not last. In 1911 Italy attacked Turkey in Tripolitania (today's Libya) in North Africa and her fleet occupied the Turkish islands of the Dodecanese in the Aegean Sea. Turkey's prestige and reform activities suffered. Russian diplomacy, since 1910 led by Sergei Sazonov (1866-1927)—Izvolsky was sent in 1910 as ambassador to Paris to strengthen the Franco-Russian alliance—became very active in the Balkans and sponsored military agreements among the four Christian Balkan kingdoms, Serbia, Bulgaria, Greece, and Montenegro. In spite of warnings by the great powers, these nations, in their own aggressive nationalism, precipitated events beyond Russia's plans. In October 1912 they attacked Turkey to "liberate" Turkish provinces with large Christian populations, principally Macedonia.

A few months later, in the Second Balkan War, the liberators fought each other bitterly over the disposition of the "liberated" regions. Out of these two wars Turkey and above all Bulgaria emerged defeated, whereas Rumania and in particular Serbia were greatly strengthened. Turkey and Bulgaria had been on the whole friendly to Austria-Hungary and Germany. The Rumanians were highly critical of the treatment suffered by their fellow Rumanians in Hungary. The Serbs relied upon Russian and French backing, not only to keep their territorial gains from the war with Turkey but also to make similar gains at the expense of Austria-Hungary. Serb aggressiveness, supported by Russian and Czech Pan-Slavism, facilitated by Austrian inertia and Magyar obstinacy, brought about the crisis of the summer of 1914. This crisis was the immediate outcome of the assassination of the heir to the throne Archduke Francis Ferdinand and his wife by a Serbian terrorist on June 28, 1914, in Sarajevo, the capital of Bosnia, where the Archduke had gone to attend the army maneuvers.

8

WAR AND DISINTEGRATION

The Widening of the War. The Austro-Hungarian government would have been in a better position if immediately after the assassination it had demanded an account of the support of the terrorists by Belgrade circles. But almost four weeks passed without any public action. Behind the scenes Count Berchtold asked whether he could count upon full German support and received an unconditional promise. The Hungarian Prime Minister, Tisza, fearful of Russian intervention and its consequences, demanded postponement of a military intervention. The President of the French Republic Raymond Poincaré visited St. Petersburg to stress Franco-Russian solidarity. On the day when he left St. Petersburg, on July 23, in the evening the Austro-Hungarian minister in Belgrade transmitted to the Serbian government a ten-point ultimatum demanding a reply within forty-eight hours. (*See Reading No. 20.*) The ultimatum was so worded that its acceptance by Serbia was hardly expected. On July 25, diplomatic relations between the two countries were broken. But only on July 28 Austria declared war on Serbia. Two days later Russia mobilized; the following day Austria-Hungary ordered general mobilization. In the first three days of August Germany sent ultimata to Russia and France and declared war on the two countries. On August 4, after Germany's invasion of Belgium, Great Britain declared war upon Germany. Only on August 5 did Austria-Hungary declare war on Russia.

Thus, what began on July 28 as a local war on Austria-Hungary's southern frontier had become, within one week, the Great European War. Nobody expected it then to last for over four years. This long duration subjected Austria-Hungary and Russia to trials far beyond their strength. Nobody foresaw, either, in August 1914 the outcome of the war, which changed fundamentally the order in central Europe and ultimately the position of even those great European powers of the nineteenth century which survived the war.

The cause of Austria-Hungary was during the war closely connected with that of the German Empire. To make the war more popular among the German workers, it was interpreted as a war against Russian despotism and thus could easily be regarded as a war of Germans against Slavs. The war aggravated everywhere nationalist passions and sanctified nationalist aspirations. The two Central Powers were later joined in the war by Turkey and Bulgaria, whereas Italy and Rumania joined the enemies of Austria-Hungary. Thus the number of nations directly involved grew far beyond the number of original participants.

The beginning of the war was unfortunate for the Austrian armies. They were defeated in Serbia and they had to abandon most of Galicia to the Russians, who later even reached the crest of the Carpathian Mountains, whence they could have descended into the Hungarian plains. But they were unable to cross the Carpathian Mountains against Austrian resistance. Austria had to carry the brunt of Russian attacks alone at the beginning of the war, because Germany concentrated her forces in the west, for a decisive break-through in France. But with the Germans halted at the Marne, the war in the west changed into a war of position and attrition. German forces were sent eastward and with their help the Austrians defeated the Russians at Gorlice and in the summer of 1915 German and Austrian troops occupied Russian Poland. By the end of 1915 the Central Powers also occupied Serbia and Montenegro.

External Victories and Domestic Difficulties. Thus at the beginning of 1916 the situation looked hopeful for the Central Powers. Austria-Hungary could throw only a part of her armed forces against Italy when the latter entered the war in May 1915, but the Italian offensive on the Isonzo River and in the South Tyrolian mountains was stopped, though with great losses on both sides. In 1916 the Austrians could even take the offensive, but they were not strong enough to sustain it. On the other hand Rumania, which entered the war against Austria in 1916, was defeated and occupied by Austrian and German troops. A victory of the Central Powers seemed within reach in 1916. German and Austro-Hungarian armies controlled much foreign territory, whereas none of their lands was under enemy occupation.

But these external victories increased the domestic difficulties of the Dual Monarchy. The war had revealed the dependence of the Habsburg monarchy on the German Empire. At the very beginning of the war most Slavs remained on the whole loyal to the monarchy. The Austrian government under the premiership of Count Carl Stürgkh (1859-1916), a mediocre bureaucrat, decided to rule without calling the Austrian parliament. The Magyars and the Austrian-Germans, convinced of the coming victory of Germany, regarded themselves more and more as the ruling races of the Habsburg monarchy and aroused among the Slavs a deep concern about their future in a German-controlled central Europe (*Mitteleuropa*).

In 1916 when Germany was militarily in the ascendant and when absolutism was in the saddle in Austria-Hungary, the Slavs could not express their fears about their future. But in 1916-17 events happened which brought about a change. Several Czech leaders, among them Dr. Karel Kramář, were sentenced to death for high treason. On October 21 an Austrian pacifist socialist, the son of the leader of the Austrian Social Democratic party, assassinated Count Stürgkh. One month later, on November 21 Emperor Francis Joseph died at his palace of Schönbrunn in the outskirts of Vienna, where he had lived the last years in practically complete retirement. External events exercised even greater pressure. The various national and social dissatisfactions of large parts of the population who suffered growing privations from the insufficient food rations were fanned by the news of the revolution of March 1917 in Russia. Their demands for democracy and national self-determination were voiced more insistently as a result of the entry of the United States into the war in April 1917. These circumstances rendered the task of the new Emperor practically hopeless.

Charles I and the Quest for Peace. Charles I (1887-1922), the last Habsburg to rule, was a nephew of Francis Ferdinand. By inclination and background he was a strictly clerical and conservative monarchist, very much influenced by Zita, princess of Bourbon-Parma, whom he had married in 1911. Neither by education nor by character was this amiable and mediocre young man equipped to deal with the rapidly developing social and political crisis. He had good intentions to achieve peace and to carry through a national settlement in the monarchy, but he had neither the strength of character nor the purposefulness to take decisive action. He pardoned Kramář and his codefendants and the Austrian parliament was recalled into session in May 1917. But the news from abroad stiffened the attitude of the nationalities and made the various proposals for a federative solution illusory.

Like Russia, Austria-Hungary needed in 1917 peace to survive. But peace was elusive in spite or perhaps because of continuing victories. The most important of them from the Austrian point of view was that of Caporetto at the end of 1917. Near this village on the Isonzo River in the Austrian province of Gorizia the Italian army was defeated and pushed back to the Piave River, which became the line of defense of the Italians. In eastern Europe the Russian and the Rumanian resistance had collapsed by that time. Austria-Hungary under its new foreign secretary, Count Ottokar Czernin (1872-1932), participated in the peace negotiations of Brest-Litovsk, which started in December 1917, and in the peace treaties concluded with the Ukraine on February 9, with Russia on March 3, and with Rumania on April 14, 1918. It was hoped that these peace treaties imposed by the Central Powers on their defeated enemies would help to alleviate the desperate food and raw material situation which prevailed above all in the big cities and in the industrial centers of the monarchy.

Charles I and Count Czernin made several attempts to arrive at a peace. The Emperor even wrote a letter on March 24, 1917, to his brother-in-law, Prince Sixtus of Bourbon-Parma who fought on the French side, declaring his readiness to support before his German allies the French "justified" claim to Alsace-Lorraine. But the Germans were still clinging to the illusion of victory and were not ready to make the necessary minimum concessions, especially in Alsace-Lorraine and Belgium. With the growing interdependence of German and Austro-Hungarian military forces during the war, an Austro-Hungarian separate peace had become impossible. Charles allowed himself to get implicated in such a move and his situation made him finally equally suspect with his German allies and with the Western Powers. As a result, the monarchy became even more dependent upon Germany, which opposed peace, and upon the Magyars, who resisted any federal reconstruction of the monarchy.

When the Austrian parliament reconvened, the Czech representatives demanded the union of Bohemia and Moravia with their Czech majorities and of Hungarian Slovakia in a single, democratic political unit. The Austrian southern Slavs similarly demanded the unification of all territories of the monarchy, including those in the Hungarian kingdom which were inhabited by Slovenes, Croats, and Serbs into one independent political unit. The Ukrainians of eastern Galicia clamored for independence from the Poles who were ruling that province. These demands ran counter to the interests of the Germans (especially in Bohemia and Moravia), of the Magyars, who wished to keep the territorial integrity of their Hungarian kingdom, and of the Poles. Meanwhile leading émigré politicians of the Czechs and the Croats had helped to arouse sympathy for Czechoslovak and Yugoslav political aims among the Western Allies.

President Woodrow Wilson in the Fourteen Points which he proclaimed on January 8, 1918, as a basis for a future peace, demanded in Point Ten that "the peoples of Austria-Hungary, whose place among the nations we wish to see safeguarded and assured, should be accorded the freest opportunity of autonomous development." This demand could be reconciled with the readiness to carry through a federal reorganization of the monarchy expressed by Emperor Charles. Two other of the Fourteen Points directly concerned the monarchy, too. Point Nine demanded that "a readjustment of the frontiers of Italy should be effected along clearly recognizable lines of nationality," and similarly Point Thirteen stipulated the erection of an independent Polish state which should include the territories inhabited by indisputably Polish populations. Neither of these points, if seriously applied, would have created insurmountable difficulties. But events overtook good intentions.

The foremost Czech representative abroad, Thomas G. Masaryk (1850-1937), a professor of philosophy at the Czech university in Prague and a member of the Austrian parliament who had left Austria in the fall of 1914 to win the Allies for the cause of Czechoslovak independence, succeeded in having Czechoslovakia recognized in 1918 as an independent and allied state with himself as head of its provisional government. Not so easy was the attempt to find a solution for the southern Slav question. The future of these peoples ran not only into the difficulty that Italy, an Allied nation, claimed much southern Slav territory in case of Allied victory, but was heavily mortgaged by the fact that the Croats and Serbs could not agree upon the form of a future united Yugoslavia. The Croat leader Ante Trumbić (1864-1938) left Austria on the eve of the war and constituted a Yugoslav committee in London. Though in the summer of 1917 in Corfu he arrived at an agreement with the Serbian government, which after being expelled from its homeland was living there in exile, the narrowly Pan-Serb attitude of the Serbian leader, Pašić, prevented a harmonious settlement between Croats and Serbs and led to many subsequent difficulties in the future Yugoslavia. All these circumstances rendered the quest for peace and for an internal reorganization of the monarchy, hesitantly initiated by Charles I, progressively more hopeless.

The End. The failure of the German offensive in France which began in March 1918 and was halted in July, and the progress of Allied forces in the Balkans destroyed the possibility for a military survival of the monarchy. A last effort to reconstruct the monarchy into federal states was made on October 16. It was drafted by a new cabinet, in which two Austrian professors, Heinrich Lammasch (1853-1920) and Joseph Redlich (1869-1936), played leading roles. Lammasch had been president of the International Court of Arbitration in the Hague and had opposed the war and the close alliance with the German Reich. But this last-minute effort of doing what the Reichstag of Kremsier had proposed in 1849 came much too late. Even then the Magyars, who showed the most stubborn misunderstanding of the trends of the time, resisted the principle of federalism and insisted on the integrity of all the lands belonging to the Holy Crown of St. Stephen. Woodrow Wilson, too, now refused to accept autonomy as the basis of peace. The Czechoslovak and the Yugoslav movements abroad proclaimed the independence of their nations. At the end of October the Czechs took over the government in Prague and the Yugoslavs in Agram, the Croatian capital. At that moment the Austro-Hungarian monarchy had for all practical purposes ceased to exist or to exercise any authority.

A few days later the Magyars and the Poles proclaimed themselves independent states too, both wishing however to retain their domination over subject peoples, the Poles over the Ukrainians, the Magyars over Slovaks and Rumanians. Even in Vienna a German-Austrian state was proclaimed. The defeated enemies of Austria-Hungary now after Austria-Hungary had collapsed pushed for an offensive. On November 4 the Italians achieved their victory of Vittorio Veneto in Venetia against an unresisting army in full disintegration, and on November 9 Rumania reëntered the war. On November 11 Emperor Charles resigned, without formal abdication, his rights to govern German Austria and on November 13, those of governing Hungary. Thus the Habsburg monarchy came to an end.

The Romanovs and the Hohenzollern preceded or accompanied the Habsburgs in their fall. Of these three dynasties the Habsburgs were by far the oldest. They had ruled in Austria since 1282 and in Hungary and Bohemia since 1526. Their fall meant not only the end of a dynasty but of a very long period in European history. For over six centuries they had embodied, as no other dynasty did, the monarchical principle.

In the nineteenth century the Habsburg monarchy had tried to adapt itself to a changing age. Its efforts were only half-hearted and often contradicted by stubborn adherence to the ways of the past. In 1815 and for some decades to follow Vienna led continental Europe as the center of the Holy Alliance which united the three conservative eastern monarchs. Little than a century later nothing remained of this alliance, its representatives and its spirit. The course and the end of the Habsburg Empire from the Napoleonic wars to the First World War were of symbolic significance for the great controversies and struggles transforming nineteenth century Europe—nationalism and national self-determination, liberalism and parliamentary institutions, federalism and constitutions, the social emancipation of peasants and of industrial workers. The monarchy was Europe's laboratory. The North-German poet and playwright Friedrich Hebbel (1813-1863), who after 1845 lived in Vienna, wrote

> This Austria is a minute world
> In which the great one stages its rehearsals.

The national anthem of the Habsburg Empire, set to a famous melody composed by Joseph Haydn in 1797, contained the line "Forever Austria's fate will be bound up with Habsburg's crown." History knows of no "forever." The lands and peoples formerly united in the Habsburg Empire went their own ways after 1918. They had quarreled in the Habsburg Empire, and their quarrels had led to a great war and the Empire's end. After that end the peoples continued to quarrel and their quarrels helped to bring about a second and greater war. Out of it emerged the Second Austrian Republic which in many ways represented the historical core of the Habsburg monarchy. Its new national anthem, set to the tune of one of Mozart's Masonic hymns, refers to the long past of Austria. When it mentions a high mission, it must be said that the monarchy was hardly aware of it and did not live up to it. But certainly the designation of Austria as a much tried land has been borne out throughout its modern history.

> Hotly contested,
> Thou liest,
> Like a strong heart,
> In the middle of the continent.
> Since the early days of the ancestors
> Thou hast borne
> The burden of high mission,
> Much tried Austria.

Part II—SELECTED READINGS

— Reading No. 1 —

METTERNICH ON CONSERVATISM[1]

In a memorandum which he wrote in 1820 for Tsar Alexander I of Russia (ruled 1801-1825) Metternich expressed his understanding of the forces struggling in Europe for the shaping of the postrevolutionary age and defended his reactionary policy.

✓   ✓   ✓

Kings have to calculate the chances of their very existence in the immediate future; passions are let loose, and league together to overthrow everything which society respects as the basis of its existence; religion, public morality, laws, customs, rights, and duties, all are attacked, confounded, overthrown, or called in question. The great mass of the people are tranquil spectators of these attacks and revolutions, and of the absolute want of all means of defence. A few are carried off by the torrent, but the wishes of the immense majority are to maintain a repose which exists no longer, and of which even the first elements seem to be lost. . . .

The scenes of horror which accompanied the first phases of the French Revolution prevented the rapid propagation of its subversive principles beyond the frontiers of France, and the wars of conquest which succeeded them gave to the public mind a direction little favorable to revolutionary principles. Thus the Jacobin propaganda failed entirely to realise criminal hopes.

Nevertheless the revolutionary seed had penetrated into

[1] From *Memoirs of Prince Metternich* (5 vols.; New York: Charles Scribner's Sons, 1881), Vol. III, pp. 455, 462 f., 465 f., 469 f., 475.

every country and spread more or less. It was greatly developed under the *régime* of the military despotism of Bonaparte. . . .

The evil exists and it is enormous. We do not think we can better define it and its cause at all times and in all places than we have already done by the word 'presumption,' that inseparable companion of the half-educated, that spring of an unmeasured ambition, and yet easy to satisfy in times of trouble and confusion.

It is principally the middle classes of society which this moral gangrene has affected, and it is only among them that the real heads of the party are found.

For the great mass of people it has no attraction and can have none. The labours to which this class—the real people—are obliged to devote themselves, are too continuous and too positive to allow them to throw themselves into vague abstractions and ambitions. The people know what is the happiest thing for them; namely, to be able to count on the morrow, for it is the morrow which will repay them for the cares and sorrows of to-day. The laws which afford a just protection to individuals, to families, and to property, are quite simple in their essence. The people dread any movement which injures industry and brings new burdens in its train. . . .

There is besides scarcely any epoch which does not offer a rallying cry to some particular faction. This cry, since 1815, has been *Constitution*. But do not let us deceive ourselves; this word, susceptible of great latitude of interpretation, would be but imperfectly understood if we supposed that the factions attached quite the same meaning to it under different *régimes*. Such is certainly not the case. In pure monarchies it is qualified by the name of 'national representation.' In countries which have lately been brought under the representative *régime* it is called 'development,' and promises charters and fundamental laws. In the only State which possesses an ancient national representation it takes 'reform' as its object. Everywhere it means change and trouble. . . .

We are convinced that society can no longer be saved without strong and vigorous resolutions on the part of the Governments still free in their opinions and actions.

We are also convinced that this may yet be, if the Governments face the truth, if they free themselves from all illusion, if they join their ranks and take their stand on a line of correct, unambiguous, and frankly announced principles.

By this course the monarchs will fulfil the duties imposed upon them by Him, who, by entrusting them with power, has charged them to watch over the maintenance of justice, and the rights of all, to avoid the paths of error, and tread firmly in the way of truth. . . .

— Reading No. 2 —

BĂLCESCU: NATIONALITY AND LIBERTY[1]

The Rumanian patriot Nicolas Bălescu emphasized in 1848 that national rights took precedence over human liberty.

✔   ✔   ✔

For my part, the question of nationality is more important than liberty. Until a people can exist as a nation, it cannot make use of liberty. Liberty can easily be recovered when it is lost [an optimism which seems rather dubious a century later], but not nationality. Therefore I believe that in the present position of our country we must aim rather at the preservation of our greatly menaced nationality and seek only as much liberty as is necessary for the development of our nationality.

[1] Quoted in Hans Kohn, *The Twentieth Century, The Challenge to the West and Its Response* (new edition; New York: The Macmillan Company, 1957), p. 15. Reprinted by permission of the publisher.

— Reading No. 3 —

THE FALL OF METTERNICH[1]

The events in Austria in March 1848 were described in the Annual Register, *a famous British publication started by Edmund Burke in 1759 to present a broad picture of the chief movements of each year. The report stressed with unusual understanding the nationality conflicts in Hungary.*

✔   ✔   ✔

We commence our narrative of the important events which happened this year in the dominions of Austria with a few remarks upon the position of Hungary, for the revolutions at Vienna had an intimate connection with the troubles which agitated that portion of the empire.

From 1812 to 1825 the Diet of Hungary had remained in a state of abeyance, and was not once convoked during that interval. . . . In 1825, the members again assembled, and from this period we may date the commencement of the aggressive attempts of the Magyar race to establish an offensive supremacy over the whole of Croatia and Slavonia. But it was not until 1830 that the Diet determined to substitute the use of the Magyar language for the Latin throughout the whole of the Slavonic population of Hungary. This awakened a strong feeling of reaction in the latter, and the joint Diet of Croatia and Slavonia, which has its sittings at Agram, the capital of Croatia, and claims to be independent of the General Hungarian Diet at Pesth, raised the cry of *"Nolumus Magyarisari;"* [We don't wish to be Magyarised]

[1] *Annual Register,* 1848, pp. 402-404.

and when at a later period the Diet at Pesth [today part of Budapest] decreed that the Magyar language should be adopted in all official transactions, and taught in the public schools, and that both the Diets should carry on their discussions in that tongue, the Croatian Diet at Agram, which had hitherto deliberated in Latin, resolved thenceforth to use the Illyrian Croatian language exclusively.

Early in March 1848 the Hungarian Chamber of Deputies assembled at Pressburg, voted an address to the Emperor, in which they, without disguise, condemned the system of Prince Metternich's policy, and advised their monarch "to surround his throne with constitutional institutions, in accordance with the ideas of the age." In this address the Chamber of Magnates also concurred. When the news of this arrived at Vienna, Prince Metternich at once proposed in the Supreme Council of State that the Hungarian Parliament should be dissolved; the announcement of which excited lively dissatisfaction in the capital.

On the 13th of March, the Diet for Lower Austria was opened, and an address was resolved upon, which contained the following passage:—

> Most Gracious Sire:—The people of Austria will elevate to the stars the Crown which, free and self-conscious, great and glorious, declares confidence to be the real fortress of the State, and harmonizes this confidence with the ideas of the age.

To this was added a petition, which asked for an immediate reform in the constitution of the Chamber, and the liberty for it forthwith to consider measures for increasing the representation; reparation of finances; and a general restoration of confidence in the empire, together with the liberty of the press.

But the people had collected in crowds around the hall, and a body of persons, consisting chiefly of students, forced their way inside. They were followed by more of the mob, and the Chamber was filled by a strange assemblage. A deputation of the States proceeded to present the address to the Emperor, and during their absence

the populace became impatient, and were very riotous;
but, when the news arrived that the requests contained
in the petition had been refused, a general destruction of
the contents of the Chamber immediately commenced.
The students headed the work of violence, and after doing
all the mischief in their power, the excited mob rushed
towards the palace, and began to attack some houses in
the immediate neighborhood. The troops now came up,
and fired in platoon upon the crowd, who however, would
not give way, and a fierce conflict took place. At last the
Burgher Guard appeared, and this produced a pause in
the struggle; but the whole body forced their way to the
palace, where they were met by the intelligence that
Prince Metternich had resigned, and that their demands
would be granted. This put a stop to the tumult, and during the night the peace of the city was preserved by the
Burgher Guard, assisted by the students, to whom arms
were supplied from the Arsenal by orders of the Government. Next morning the troops of the line, to the
number of 18,000, were withdrawn beyond the walls,
and the preservation of order was confided to the Burgher
Guard. The formation of a National Guard was also
decreed. On the 15th, the following important proclamation was issued by the Emperor.

> By virtue of our declaration abolishing the censorship,
> liberty of the press is allowed in the form under which
> it exists in those countries which have hitherto enjoyed
> it. A National Guard, established on the basis of prop-
> erty and intelligence, already performs the most bene-
> ficial service.

> The necessary steps have been taken for convoking,
> with the least possible loss of time, the Deputies from
> all our provincial States, and from the Central Congre-
> gations of the Lombardo-Venetian kingdom, (the repre-
> sentation of the class of burghers being strengthened,
> and due regard being paid to the existing provincial
> constitutions,) in order that they may deliberate on the
> constitution which we have resolved to grant to our
> people.

> We therefore confidently expect that excited tempers
> will become composed, that study will resume its wonted
> course, and that industry and peaceful intercourse will
> spring into new life.

Prince Metternich fled from Vienna, and ultimately took up his abode in England—the great land of refuge this year for distressed foreigners. A Provisional Council was in the meantime appointed. . . . In the midst of all this confusion and excitement, the people gave a proof that the inherent loyalty of the German character was by no means extinct, for when the Emperor, surrounded by several members of the Imperial Family, appeared on the balcony of the Court Library, on the Joseph Platz, where the National Guard was drawn up in ranks, they were received with enthusiastic shouts. Suddenly the National Anthem was begun, and the effect upon the assembled multitude was electric. Tears flowed down the cheeks of young and old, and it seemed as if the Crown had never been more endeared to the people.

— Reading No. 4 —

METTERNICH: A MODERN VIEW[1]

Metternich was regarded with sharp disapproval in the nineteenth century, the century of rising nationalism. His significance is better seen today as the last representative of a prenationalist Europe. The following characterization was written by Henry A. Kissinger, a young American scholar, in 1956.

⸎   ⸎   ⸎

What enabled Metternich to emerge as the Prime Minister of Europe? It was Metternich's misfortune that history in the latter half of the nineteenth century was written by his opponents, to whom he was anathema both by principle and policy, and who ascribed his achievements to a contradictory combination of cunning and good fortune, of mediocrity and incompetent adversaries, without explaining how such a man managed to place his stamp on his period. For the documents of his period leave no doubt that for over a generation nothing occurred in Europe which was not shaped by Metternich either directly or through his opposition. . . . On the other hand, Metternich's own interpretation of the superiority of his philosophical maxims is refuted by their conventionality, while mere deviousness could not have duped all of Europe for over a decade. Rather, Metternich's successes were due to two factors: that the unity of Europe was not Metternich's invention, but the common conviction of *all* statesmen; and because Metternich

[1] Henry A. Kissinger, *A World Restored* (Boston: Houghton Mifflin, 1957), pp. 319-322. Reprinted by permission.

was the last diplomat of the great tradition of the eighteenth century, a "scientist" of politics, unemotionally arranging his combinations in an age increasingly conducting policy by "causes." . . . And because, despite his vanity, he was always ready to sacrifice the form of a settlement for the substance, his victories became, not wounds, but definitions of a continuing relationship.

Metternich had the great advantage over his adversaries that he knew what he wanted; and if his goals were sterile, they were fixed. . . . But all his diplomatic skill would have availed him nothing, had he not operated in a framework in which his invocation of the unity of Europe could appear as something other than a euphemism for Austrian national interest. The early nineteenth century was a transition period, and, as in all such periods, the emergence of a new pattern of obligation for a time served only to throw into sharp relief the values being supplanted. . . . To Metternich's contemporaries the unity of Europe was a reality. Regional differences were recognized, but they were considered local variations of a greater whole. . . . All of Metternich's colleagues . . . understood each other, not only because they could converse with facility in French, but because in a deeper sense they were conscious that the things they shared were much more fundamental than the issues separating them. . . . If Metternich had any special ties to Austria, they derived from a philosophical not a national identification, because the principles Austria represented were closest to his own maxims, because Austria, the polyglot empire, was a microcosm of his cosmopolitan or European values. "For a long time now," he wrote to Wellington in 1824, "Europe has had for me the quality of a fatherland."

For these reasons, Metternich was effective because he was plausible. Of all his colleagues he was best able to appeal to the maxims of the eighteenth century, partly because they corresponded to his own beliefs, but more importantly because Austria's interests were identical with those of European repose. . . . Metternich's policy was thus a policy of status quo *par excellence,* and conducted, not by marshalling a superior force, but by obtaining a voluntary submission to his version of legitimacy. Its achievement was a period of peace lasting for over a generation without armament races or even the threat of a major war.

But its failure was the reverse side of this success. The identification of stability with the status quo in the middle of a revolutionary period reinforced the tendency towards rigidity of Austria's domestic structure and led eventually to its petrifaction. The very dexterity of Metternich's diplomacy obscured the real nature of his achievements, that he was merely hiding the increasing anachronism of Austria in a century of nationalism and liberalism; that he was but delaying the inevitable day of reckoning. . . . The end of the Napoleonic war marked the last moment for Austria to attempt to brave the coming storm by adaptation, to wrench itself loose from the past, however painful the process. But Metternich's marvellous diplomatic skill enabled Austria to avoid the hard choice between domestic reform and revolutionary struggle; to continue a multi-national empire in a period of nationalism. So agile was Metternich's performance that it was forgotten that its basis was diplomatic skill and that it left the fundamental problems unsolved, that it was manipulation and not creation.

— Reading No. 5 —

PALACKY: LETTER TO THE GERMAN NATIONAL ASSEMBLY[1]

On April 11, 1848, Palacký expressed in a letter to the German National Assembly in Frankfort, which had invited him to participate as a Czech delegate, the principles why he could not participate and formulated the principles of the Czech and Slav national policy in the Habsburg Empire.

✦   ✦   ✦

I am a Czech of Slav descent and with all the little I own and possess I have devoted myself wholly and for ever to the service of my nation. That nation is small, it is true, but from time immemorial it has been an independent nation with its own character; its rulers have participated since old times in the federation of German princes, but the nation never regarded itself nor was it regarded by others throughout all the centuries, as part of the German nation. The whole union of the Czech lands first with the Holy German Empire and then with the German Confederation was always a purely dynastic one of which the Czech nation, the Czech Estates, hardly wished to know and which they hardly noticed. . . .

If anyone asks that the Czech nation should now unite with the German nation, beyond this heretofore existing

[1] Translated and quoted in Hans Kohn, *Pan-Slavism, Its History and Ideology* (Notre Dame University Press, 1953), pp. 65-69. Printed with the permission of the publisher.

federation between princes, this is then a new demand which has no historical legal basis, a demand to which I personally do not feel justified in acceding until I receive an express and valid mandate for it. The second reason which prevents me from participating in your deliberations is the fact that from all that has been so far publicly announced of your aims and purposes you irrevocably are, and will be, aiming to undermine Austria forever as an independent empire and to make its existence impossible—an empire whose preservation, integrity and consolidation is, and must be, a great and important matter not only for my own nation but for the whole of Europe, indeed for mankind and civilization itself. Allow me kindly to explain myself briefly on this point.

You know, gentlemen, what power it is that holds the whole great eastern part of our continent; you know that this power which now already has grown to vast dimensions, increases and expands by its own strength every decade to a far greater extent than is possible in the Western countries; that being inaccessible at its own center to almost every attack, it has become, and has for a long time been, a threat to its neighbours; and that, although it has an open access to the north, is nevertheless always seeking, led by natural instinct, to expand southwards and will continue to do it; that every further step which it will take forward on this path threatens at an ever accelerated pace to produce and found a *universal monarchy*, that is to say, an infinite and inexpressible evil, a misfortune without measure or bound which I, though heart and soul a Slav, would nonetheless deeply regret for the good of mankind even though that monarchy proclaimed itself a Slav one.

Many people in Russia call and regard me as an enemy of the Russians, with as little justice as those who among the Germans regard me as an enemy of the Germans. I proclaim loudly and publicly that I am in no way an enemy of the Russians: on the contrary, I observe with joyful sympathy every step by which this great nation within its natural borders progresses along the road of civilization: but with all my ardent love of my nation I always esteem more highly the good of mankind and of learning than the good of the nation; for this reason the bare possibility of a Russian universal monarchy has no more determined opponent or adversary than myself, not because that monarchy would be Russian but because it would be universal.

You know that in south-east Europe, along the frontiers of the Russian empire, there live many nations widely different in origin, language, history and habits— Slavs, Rumanians, Magyars, and Germans, not to speak of Greeks, Turks and Albanians—none of whom is strong enough by itself to be able to resist successfully for all time the superior neighbour to the east; they could do it only if a close and firm tie bound them all together. The vital artery of this necessary union of nations is the Danube; the focus of its power must never be removed far from this river, if the union is to be effective at all and to remain so. Certainly, if the Austrian state had not existed for ages, we would be obliged in the interests of Europe and even of mankind to endeavor to create it as fast as possible.

But why have we seen this state, which by nature and history is destined to be the bulwark and guardian of Europe against Asiatic elements of every kind—why have we seen it in a critical moment helpless and almost unadvised in the face of the advancing storm? It is because in an unhappy blindness which has lasted for very long, Austria has not recognized the real legal and moral foundation of its existence and has denied it: the fundamental rule that all the nationalities united under its scepter should enjoy complete equality of rights and respect. The right of nations is truly a natural right; no nation on earth has the right to demand that its neighbour should sacrifice itself for its benefit, no nation obliged to deny or sacrifice itself for the good of its neighbour.

Nature knows neither ruling nor subservient nations. If the union which unites several different nations is to be firm and lasting, no nation must have cause to fear that by that union it will lose any of the goods which it holds most dear; on the contrary each must have the certain hope that it will find in the central authority defense and protection against possible violations of equality by neighbours; then every nation will do its best to strengthen that central authority so that it can successfully provide the aforesaid defense. I am convinced that even now it is not too late for the Austrian empire to proclaim openly and sincerely this fundamental rule of justice, the *sacra ancora* for a ship in danger of floundering, and to carry it out energetically in common and in every respect: but every moment is precious; for God's sake do not let us delay another hour with this! . . .

When I look behind the Bohemian frontiers, then natural and historical reasons make me turn not to Frankfurt but to Vienna to seek there the center which is fitted and destined to ensure and defend the peace, the liberty and the right of my nation. Your efforts, gentlemen, seem to me now to be directed as I have already stated, not only towards ruinously undermining, but even utterly destroying that center from whose might and strength I expect the salvation not only of the Czech land. . . .

And if Hungary following its instincts severs its connections with the (Austrian) state or, what would amount almost to the same, concentrates within itself—will then Hungary which does not wish to hear of national equality within its borders be able to maintain itself free and strong in the future? Only the just is truly free and strong. A voluntary union of the Danubian Slavs and Rumanians, or even of the Poles themselves, with such a state which declares that a man must first be a Magyar before he can be a human being is entirely out of the question; and even less thinkable would be a compulsory union of this kind. . . .

"In conclusion I must briefly express my conviction that those who ask that Austria (and with it Bohemia) should unite on national lines with the German empire, demand its suicide. . . . Nothing remains for the Austrian and German Empires but to organize themselves side by side on a footing of equality, to convert the existing ties into a permanent alliance of defense and defiance, and should it be advantageous to both sides perhaps to create also a customs union. I am ready at every moment gladly to give a helping hand in all activities which do not endanger the independence, integrity and growth in power of the Austrian empire."

— Reading No. 6 —

GERMAN RADICALS AGAINST SLAV NATIONALISM[1]

After the suppression of the Czech national revolution of 1848 by Prince Windischgrätz, the German radical revolutionaries openly expressed their joy. The Viennese radical Volksfreund (The People's Friend) *commented in its issue of June 24, 1848.*

✓   ✓   ✓

The events in Prague, on the whole, seem to have confused the public and the newspapers all the more since the battle has ended and there is no longer any possibility that fighting will again break out. The Czechs (when we say Czechs we mean the insane or corrupt Slav party of the Czechs, which, in union with another insane and corrupt party, has designs on turning and uses every conceivable means—even a barbaric union with Russia if it would be necessary—to turn Austria into a Slav empire, at the expense of the Germans and Hungarians) this Slav party has been defeated on the field of battle, and Windischgrätz has remained the victor. Because of the great and justified embitterment of all Germans over the Slavic association of lunatics in Prague, the prospects have become great since his victory that Windischgrätz may even become a popular and much-loved man, for people suspect the wild, hate-brewing, fear-inspiring doings of the Czech party, with all their armed Swornost

[1] Quoted and translated by R. John Rath, *The Viennese Revolution of 1848* (Austin: University of Texas Press, 1957), pp. 262 f. Reprinted by permission of the publisher.

League, too much not to be happy that a powerful fist has finally given this party a death blow.

We must not, therefore, be surprised over the satisfaction that was first expressed over Prince Windischgrätz's victory. This satisfaction was universal, and the Volksfreund shared in it and still does. For this victory can be decisive, not only for the fate of the Germans in Prague and in all Bohemia, but for the fate of all Bohemia, if it is sensibly used in a spirit of freedom and if the corpses of the defeated Czech party have served to avert a civil war. Furthermore, the victory in Prague can have the best consequences, not only for Bohemia, but also for Hungary and Transylvania and for the whole monarchy, for we know only too well how a victory for the Czech party would have encouraged, intoxicated, and spurred on to the utmost degree all the Slavs in the monarchy. The victory over the Czech party in Prague is and remains a joyful event. A victory for German concerns in Bohemia and in the monarchy can never be a misfortune, for the Germans bring humanity and freedom to the conquered. A small, defeated party like the Czechs, over against whom there will always be forty million Germans, can be well satisfied with this price. Whether Windischgrätz fought in the name of and for German matters is another question. It is a question over which the opinions of our newspapers are now divided. Unfortunately most of them have fallen into the error of assuming that Windischgrätz has all of a sudden become a hero and a front-rank fighter for the party of retrogression (reaction).

— Reading No. 7 —

CROATIAN ASPIRATIONS FOR AUTONOMY[1]

On March 25, 1848, the representatives of the Triune Kingdom of Croatia, Slavonia, and Dalmatia assembled in Agram (Zagreb), the capital of Croatia, and adopted a declaration representing the typical nationalist and constitutional liberal demands of the period.

✓ ✓ ✓

The nations of the Triune Kingdom, animated by the desire of continuing, as heretofore, under the Hungarian crown, with which the free crown of Croatia, Slavonia, and Dalmatia was voluntarily united by their ancestors; animated by the desire of remaining true to the reigning dynasty, which at present rules the land according to the Pragmatic Sanction; and, finally, animated by the desire of maintaining the integrity of the Austrian monarchy, and that of the kingdom of Hungary, while they at the same time are anxious to uphold those great boons which were obtained for the whole Austrian empire during the three bloody and important days of the 12th, 13th, and 14th of March, making the following demands upon the king's sense of justice:

1. The extraordinary position in which the nation finds itself, as well as the restoration of its legal order, requires an authorized head; and with this view it has unanimously elected Baron Joseph Jelačić principal magistrate of the three united kingdoms, a man who pos-

[1] William H. Stiles, *Austria 1848-49* (New York: Harper & Brothers, 1852), pp. 379-381.

sesses the confidence of the whole nation, and wishes that the command of the frontier troops, and the right of calling together the Diet, may also be granted to him.

2. That the Diet of these kingdoms be summoned to meet at Agram by May the 1st of this year at the latest.

3. A strong and new union, in every respect of the kingdom of Dalmatia, which by tradition and by law belongs to us, with the kingdoms of Croatia and Slavonia, and the incorporation of all other parts of our country, which in the course of time have become lost to us and united with the Hungarian counties and the Austrian provinces.

4. Their national independence.

5. Their own independent ministry, responsible to the Diet of these kingdoms, whose members shall consist of men of popular opinions, and devoted to the more modern tendencies toward freedom and progress.

6. The introduction of the national language into the interior and exterior administration of these kingdoms, as well as into all establishments for public instruction.

7. The foundation of a university at Agram.

8. Political and intellectual development on the principles of a free national spirit.

9. Freedom of press, creeds, instruction, and speech.

10. A yearly Diet at Agram, Eszeg [Osijek in Slavonia], Zara [in Dalmatia], and Fiume, in turns.

11. The representation of the people on the principle of equality, without reference to rank, for the approaching as well as all future Croatian, Dalmatian, and Slavonian Diets.

12. Equality of all in the sight of the law, as well as publicity in law proceedings, together with a jury and responsibility of the judges.

13. Proportionate taxation upon all classes, without regard to rank.

14. Exemption from all compulsory labor and "corvée."

15. Establishment of a national bank.

16. Restoration of our national funds, which hitherto

have been under Hungarian management, as well as of all properties and funds belonging to the finance department. The above to be managed by a responsible finance minister.

17. A National Guard, the command of which to be vested in the "lands captain," chosen by the Diet, according to the old custom.

18. The national troops of every description, in times of peace, to remain in the country; the officers to be natives, and the word of command to be given in the national language; in times of war, or of observation of a foreign enemy, viz., upon frontier duty, the troops to receive food, pay, and clothing. All foreign troops to leave the country.

19. The national troops to swear fidelity to the common Constitution, their King, and the freedom of their nation, and of all other free nations composing the Austrian monarchy, according to the principles of humanity.

20. All political prisoners, whether in the Triune Kingdom or in other free provinces of Austria to be set at liberty.

21. Right of association, assembly and petition.

22. Abolition of all customhouses upon the frontiers of our country . . . and proclamation of reciprocal free trade.

27. The town and country communes of the country to be organized upon the principles of liberty, with the right of self-government and freedom of speech.

28. The old names for the lieutenants of counties, "zupanie," to be resumed, and they themselves to be organized according to old customs, but in the spirit of modern freedom.

29. All offices, without exception, temporal as well as spiritual, to be vested exclusively in natives of the Triune Kingdom.

30. Abolition of celibacy in the Church, and the use of the native language in Church service, according to the old Croatian rights and customs.

— Reading No. 8 —

THE PEASANTRY IN AUSTRIA AND IN HUNGARY AFTER 1848[1]

The year 1848 marked a definite improvement of the economic and social conditions of the peasants in Austria but not in Hungary. The following descriptions taken from a British source present an authoritative picture.

✔   ✔   ✔

The abolition of the feudal burdens upon land which Mr. Fyffe has described as "almost the sole gain that Austria derived from the struggle in 1848," practically transformed the small peasant farmers into independent proprietors. The immediate effect of the cessation of compulsory villein service (Frohne) was to hasten the transition from a system of home production (Naturalwirtschaft), regulated by custom, to the modern system of competitive production based upon money exchanges (Geldwirtschaft). The great proprietors, unprovided with the capital necessary to enable them to hire farm hands to supply the place of the labourers of whose traditional service they had been deprived, found themselves obliged to divide their demesne lands into small holdings, which were leased out to their former feudal dependents (Unterthänige Bauern). In this way the conversion of home farms worked by a bailiff into leaseholds let out for a

[1] Great Britain, *Parliamentary Papers.* The Royal Commission on Labour. Foreign Reports, vol. XI (1893-94), pp. 72, 173 f.

money-rent to tenant farmers, which had begun even
before 1848, became very general in Austria, though
opinions are still divided as to which of the two methods
of cultivation is really the more successful and economi-
cal. Large manorial estates or latifundia are chiefly found
in Bohemia, which has been called "the stronghold of
the feudal aristocracy," and in Galicia, Moravia, and
Lower Austria. They are very rare in Carinthia and
Salzburg, and in Dalmatia, where the large properties
are chiefly in the hands of the merchant or capitalist
class, they are practically unknown. . . .

It is partly the conservative tendency of the large
landowners, partly the dread of reform shown by the
peasantry which has hitherto prevented progress in agricultural matters in Hungary. The history of Hungary
affords only a single instance of an uprising of discontented peasantry against the nobles; this was in 1514 and
the consequences were a strong repression and im-
position of heavier burdens. Free migration was pro-
hibited and the peasants became and remained serfs
(Leibeigene) until 1848 when the right of life and death
(jus gladii) of the nobles over them was finally abolished;
this account should be taken together with that of Mr.
Patterson who shows, as will be seen presently, that
whatever the theoretical claims of the nobles may have
been, the peasantry had acquired certain rights over the
land through various causes, but particularly through the
Government claims on the land and its jealousy towards
the nobles. The great changes of 1848, which were perhaps most striking in political life, were certainly also
remarkable and extended in the agricultural sphere, but
the final abolition of privilege in acquisition and free
disposition of landed property must not be considered as
wholly sudden or violent. The very privilege of the
nobles in exemption from taxation gave the government a
special interest in the tax-paying classes or peasants settled
on "non-noble" land. Noble land was not necessarily occupied by nobles; they often let it out in allotments to
peasant tenants called contractualists or curialists to distinguish them from older tenants called jobbagyones, or,
after the survey of Maria Theresa in 1767-73 (Urbar-

ium), urbarialists. Both classes of tenants had certain rights and it would be a mistake to consider the dues paid by the latter to the noble landlord as simply feudal dues. The forced labour (robot) and payments in money and kind were determined by "immemorial custom," and although, while the contractualist paid only a capitation tax, the urbarialist had to pay both a capitation and a land-tax, yet the latter gained through the anxiety of the Government to keep up the number of taxpayers and the area of taxable land. The government "regarded with extreme suspicion the conduct of the lord towards the peasantry. He was not allowed to evict them except for certain definite reasons set down in the law. The copyholds were hereditary and should the copyholding family die out or be evicted, the lord was not allowed to occupy the holding but was obliged to give it to another non-noble tenant." These holdings were fixed as to extent in given districts although they were larger in some districts than in others. . . .

In 1848 these "copyhold" farms were transformed by the Hungarian liberals into freehold estates, but even before this date many landlords had enabled their tenants "to buy their freedom at a moderate price," thus preparing the public mind for general measures of emancipation. The position of the contractualists was different from that of the urbarialists, and it was mainly due to the troubled times that followed the Reform Bill of 1848, that a confusion arose between the two forms of tenure, a confusion which tended to operate to the advantage of the peasant holder and disadvantage of the landlord. Mr. Patterson affirmed in 1869 that while there would be no doubt as to the permanent advantage to the country at large of the emancipation of the peasant lands, there could be "as little doubt that the class of the noble landlords suffered severely, as the great majority of them were perfectly unprepared for the change. In the slovenly system of agriculture which was fostered in both lord and peasant by the institution of robot or forced labour, which formed the greater portion of the rent of these copyhold farms, the lord had not only no experience of what paying regular wages meant,

but he had not even draught cattle or agricultural imple-
ments." The Government bonds bearing interest, which
were given him in compensation for his losses, were
thrown in large masses on the money market and sold
considerably below their value. The pecuniary losses
which followed through the war of Independence, subsequent defeat and enforced military service still further
crippled the Hungarian landlords.

Out of these circumstances, thus briefly sketched, arose
a serious agricultural crisis during which the chief difficulties to be fought were those which met the large and
middle-sized properties whilst the peasants suffered com-
paratively little owing to their increased control of their
holdings which they worked with the assistance of their
families. On the other hand the large proprietors (Lati-
fundienbesitzer) were able to command the credit which
enabled them to tide over the period. This was not so
with the smaller or middle-class proprietors; suddenly
bereft of the sole means known to them of cultivating
their lands and unable to resort to local credit, a system
which was practically unknown in Hungary, and which
indeed is even now far from being satisfactorily developed; destitute of technical knowledge and hitherto
more occupied with local politics than rural economy;
engaged in a struggle with the absolutism of the Austrian
Government, a large number of them found themselves
face to face with ruin. Exact statistics are lacking during
the first part of this period for the relative position of
the various properties, but there is no doubt that from
this time a process of transfer set in, which is not yet
concluded, whereby the largest and the smallest holdings have increased at the expense of the middle class
holdings.

— Reading No. 9 —

HUNGARIAN DECLARATION OF INDEPENDENCE[1]

On April 14, 1849, the Hungarian Diet meeting in the Protestant Church at Debreczin (Debrecen) in eastern Hungary adopted after an address by Kossuth the following Declaration of Independence.

✓   ✓   ✓

We, the legally constituted representatives of the Hungarian nation assembled in the Diet, do by these presents solemnly proclaim and maintain the inalienable natural rights of Hungary with all its dependencies, to occupy the position of an independent European State—that the House of Habsburg Lorraine, as perjured in the sight of God and man, has forfeited its right to the Hungarian throne. At the same time, we feel ourselves bound in duty to make known the motives and reasons which have impelled us to this decision, that the civilized world may learn we have taken this step, not out of overweening confidence in our own wisdom, or out of revolutionary excitement, but that it is an act of the last necessity, adopted to preserve from destruction a nation persecuted to the limits of the most enduring patience.

Three hundred years have passed since the Hungarian nation, by free election, placed the House of Austria upon its throne, in accordance with stipulations made on both sides, and ratified by treaty. These three hundred

[1] E.O.S., *Hungary and Its Revolutions From the Earliest Period to the Nineteenth Century* (London: George Bell and Sons, 1896), pp. 431-433.

years have been a period of uninterrupted suffering for the country.

The Creator has blessed this land with all the elements of wealth and happiness. Its area of 100,000 square miles presents, in varied profusion, innumerable sources of prosperity. Its population numbering nearly fifteen millions feels the glow of youthful strength within its veins, and has shewn temper and docility which guarantee its proving at once the mainspring of civilization in Eastern Europe, and the guardian of that civilization when attacked. Never was a more grateful task appointed to a reigning dynasty by the dispensation of Divine Providence, than that which devolved upon the House of Habsburg Lorraine. If nothing had been done to impede the development of the country Hungary would now rank amongst the most prosperous of nations. It was only necessary to refrain from curtailing the moderate share of Constitutional liberty which the Hungarians united with rare fidelity to their Sovereigns, and cautiously maintained through the troubles of a thousand years, and the House of Habsburg might long have counted this nation amongst the most faithful adherents to the throne.

But this dynasty which cannot point to a single ruler who has based his power on the freedom of the people, adopted, from generation to generation a course towards this nation which meets the name of perjury. . . .

Confiding in the justice of an eternal God, we in the face of the civilized world, in reliance upon the natural rights of the Hungarian nation and upon the power it has developed to maintain them, further impelled by that sense of duty which urges every nation to defend its own existence, do hereby declare and proclaim in the name of the nation, lawfully represented by us, as follows:—

1st. Hungary with Transylvania, as by law united, with its dependencies, are hereby declared to constitute a free independent Sovereign state. The territorial unity of this State is declared to be inviolable, and its territory to be indivisible.

2nd. The House of Habsburg Lorraine, having by

treachery, perjury, and levying war against the Hungarian nation, as well as by its outrageous violation of all compacts, in breaking up the integral territory of the kingdom, in the separation of Transylvania, Croatia, Sclavonia, Fiume, and its districts from Hungary; further, by compassing the destruction of the independence of the country by arms, and by calling in the disciplined army of a foreign power for the purpose of annihilating its nationality . . . —is, as treacherous and perjured, for ever excluded from the throne of the United States of Hungary and Transylvania, and all their possessions and dependencies, and is hereby deprived of the style and title, as well as of the armorial bearings belonging to the Crown of Hungary, and declared to be banished for ever from the united countries, and their dependencies and possessions.

3rd. The Hungarian nation, in the exercise of its rights and sovereign will, being determined to assume the position of a free and independent State amongst the nations of Europe, declares it to be its intention to establish and maintain friendly and neighbourly relations with those States with which it was formerly united under the same Sovereign, as well as to contract alliances with all other nations.

4th. The form of government to be adopted in future will be fixed by the Diet of the Nation. . . .

And this resolution of ours we shall proclaim and make known to all the nations of the civilized world, with the conviction, that the Hungarian nation will be received by them amongst free and independent nations, with the same friendship and free acknowledgement of its rights, which the Hungarians proffer to other countries. . . .

— Reading No. 10 —

THE AUSTRO-HUNGARIAN COMPROMISE OF 1867[1]

The Compromise (Ausgleich) of October 1867 changed the Austrian monarchy into the Austro-Hungarian monarchy. The complicated relationship between the two parts of the Habsburg Empire was governed by two almost identical laws, one accepted by Austria, the other by Hungary. The more important stipulations of the Austrian law are given below.

❧   ❧   ❧

ARTICLE 1. The following affairs are declared common to Austria and Hungary:

a. Foreign affairs, including diplomatic and commercial representation abroad, as well as measures relating to international treaties, reserving the right of the representative bodies of both parts of the empire [Reichsrat and Hungarian Diet] to approve such treaties, in so far as such approval is required by the Constitution.

b. Military and naval affairs; excluding the voting of contingents and legislation concerning the manner of performing military service, the provisions relative to the local disposition and maintenance of the army, the civil relations of persons belonging to the army, and their rights and duties in matters not pertaining to the military service.

c. The finances, with reference to matters of common

[1] Herbert F. Wright, ed., *The Constitution of the States at War, 1914-1918* (Washington, D.C.: Government Printing Office, 1919), pp. 4-10.

expense, especially the establishment of the budget and the examination of accounts.

ART. 2. Besides these, the following affairs shall not indeed be administered in common, but shall be regulated upon uniform principles to be agreed upon from time to time:

1. Commercial affairs, especially customs legislation.

2. Legislation concerning indirect taxes which stand in close relation to industrial production.

3. The establishment of a monetary system and monetary standards.

4. Regulations concerning railway lines which affect the interests of both parts of the empire.

5. The establishment of a system of defense.

ART. 3. The expenses of affairs common to both Austria and Hungary shall be borne by the two parts of the empire in proportion to be fixed from time to time by an agreement between the two legislative bodies (Reichsrat and Diet), approved by the emperor. If an agreement can not be reached between the two representative bodies, the proportion shall be fixed by the emperor, but for the term of one year only. The method of defraying its quota of the common expense shall belong exclusively to each of the parts of the empire.

Nevertheless, joint loans may be made for affairs of common interest; in such a case all that relates to the negotiation of the loan, as well as the method of employing and repaying it, shall be determined in common.

The decision as to whether a joint loan shall be made is reserved for legislation by each of the two parts of the empire.

ART. 4. The contribution towards the expense of the present public debt shall be determined by an agreement between the two parts of the empire.

ART. 5. The administration of common affairs shall be conducted by a joint responsible ministry, which is forbidden to direct at the same time the administration of joint affairs and those of either part of the empire.

The regulation of the management, conduct, and internal organization of the joint army shall belong exclusively to the emperor.

Art. 6. The legislative power belonging to the legislative bodies of each of the two parts of the empire [Reichsrat and Hungarian Diet] shall be exercised by them, in so far as it relates to joint affairs, by means of delegations.

Art. 7. The delegation from the Reichsrat shall consist of 60 members, of whom one third shall be taken from the House of Lords and two thirds from the House of Representatives. . . .

Art. 10. Delegates and their substitutes shall be elected annually by the two houses of the Reichsrat.

The delegates and substitutes shall retain their functions until the new election.

Members of the delegation are eligible for reelection.

Art. 11. The delegations shall be convened annually by the emperor, who shall determine the place of their meeting. . . .

Art. 13. The powers of the delegations shall extend to all matters concerning common affairs.

All other matters shall be beyond their power.

Art. 14. The projects of the government shall be submitted by the joint ministry to each of the delegations separately.

Each delegation shall also have the right to submit projects concerning affairs which are within its competence.

Art. 15. For the passage of a law concerning matters within the power of the delegations the agreement of both delegations shall be necessary, or in default of such agreement, a vote of the full assembly of the two delegations sitting together; in either case the approval of the emperor shall be necessary.

Art. 16. The right to hold the joint ministry to its responsibility shall be exercised by the delegations.

In case of the violation of a constitutional law in force regarding common affairs, either of the delegations may present charges to the other against the joint ministry or against any one of its members.

The impeachment shall be legally effective when resolved upon separately by each of the delegations, or in a joint meeting of the two. . . .

ART. 19. Each delegation shall act, deliberate and vote in separate session. Article 31 indicates an exception to this rule.

ART. 20. The decisions of the delegation of the Reichsrat shall require for their validity the presence of not less than 30 members besides the president, and every decision shall require the vote of a majority of those present.

ART. 21. The delegates and substitutes from the Reichsrat shall receive no instructions from their electors. . . .

ART. 27. The session of the delegation shall be closed, after the completion of its work, by the president with the consent of the emperor or by his order.

ART. 28. The members of the joint ministry shall have the right to take part in all deliberations of the delegation, and to present their projects personally or through a deputy.

They shall be heard whenever they desire.

The delegation shall have the right to address questions to the joint ministry or to any one of its members, to require answers and explanations and to appoint committees to whom the ministers shall furnish all necessary information.

ART. 29. The sessions of the delegation shall be as a rule public.

Exceptionally the public may be excluded if it is so decided by the assembly in secret session, upon the request of the president or of not less than five members.

Every decision, however, shall be made in public session.

ART. 30. Each delegation shall communicate to the other its decisions and, if the case requires it, the reasons therefor.

This communication shall take place in writing, in German on the part of the delegation of the Reichsrat, in the Hungarian language on the part of the delegation of the Diet; in each case there shall be annexed a certified translation into the language of the other delegation.

ART. 31. Each delegation shall have the right to propose that a question be decided by a vote in joint session, and this proposal can not be declined by the other delegation after the exchange of three written communications without result.

The two presidents shall agree upon the time and place of the joint meeting of the two delegations for the purpose of voting together.

ART. 32. In the joint sessions the presidents of the delegations shall preside alternately. It shall be determined by lot which of the two presidents shall preside in the first place.

In all subsequent sessions the presidency at the first joint meeting shall belong to the present of the delegation which has not had the presidency at the meeting immediately preceding.

ART. 33. In order to transact business in joint session the presence of not less than two thirds of the members of each delegation shall be necessary.

Decisions shall be reached by a majority vote.

If one delegation has more members present than the other, so many members shall abstain from voting as shall be necessary to establish an equality of the number of voters from each delegation.

It shall be determined by lot which members shall abstain from voting.

ART. 34. The joint sessions of the two delegations shall be public.

The minutes shall be kept in two languages by the secretaries of the two delegations and attested by both.

ART. 35. Further details regarding the procedure of the delegation of the Reichsrat shall be regulated by an order of business to be adopted by the delegation itself.

ART. 36. Agreement concerning matters which, though not managed in common, yet are to be regulated upon the same principles, shall be reached in one of the following ways: (1) The responsible ministries by an agreement between themselves shall prepare a project of law which shall be submitted to the representative bodies of the two parts of the empire and the project agreed upon by the two representative bodies shall be submitted for the approval of the emperor. (2) Each representative body shall elect from its members a deputation composed of an equal number of members, which shall prepare a project upon the initiative of the respective ministries; such project shall be submitted to each of the legislative bodies by the ministries, shall be regularly considered, and the identical law of the two assemblies shall be submitted for the approval of the emperor. The second procedure shall be followed especially in reaching an agreement concerning the distribution of the cost of affairs administered in common.

— Reading No. 11 —

A STATISTICAL SURVEY OF THE AUSTRO-HUNGARIAN MONARCHY[1]

After 1867 the Habsburg Empire consisted of two sovereign states loosely associated for certain common affairs. With the river Leitha, a tributary of the Danube, forming a section of the boundary between the western and the eastern parts of the Empire, one calls them also Cisleithania and Transleithania. Their divisions and populations according to the last census taken, the one of 1910, were as follows.

↗   ↗   ↗

I. In 1910 the population of the three parts of the Habsburg Empire was the following:

Austria	28,572,000
Hungary	20,886,000
Bosnia-Herzegovina	1,932,000
Total of the Habsburg Empire	51,390,000

II. THE DIVISIONS OF CISLEITHANIA. The western half of the empire had no official name. It was designated as "The kingdoms and lands represented in the *Reichstag.*" These historical provinces were the following:

---

[1] For critical remarks on Austro-Hungarian statistics and their evaluation see Robert A. Kann, *The Multinational Empire, Nationalism and National Reform in the Habsburg Monarchy 1848-1918* (New York: Columbia University Press, 1950), Vol. II, pp. 299-308.

1. The Habsburg hereditary lands: the Archduchy of Lower Austria; the Archduchy of Upper Austria; the Duchy of Styria (Steiermark); the Duchy of Carinthia (Kärnten); the Duchy of Carniola (Krain); the Princely County of Tyrol; the Land of Vorarlberg; the Duchy of Salzburg.

2. The Lands of the Crown of St. Wenceslaus: the Kingdom of Bohemia; the Margravate of Moravia; the Duchy of Upper and Lower Silesia.

3. The lands north of the Carpathian Mountains: the Kingdom of Galicia and Lodomeria, with the Grand Duchy of Cracow; the Duchy of Bukovina.

4. The Adriatic Lands: the Margravate of Istria; the Princely County of Görz and Gradiska; the City of Trieste; the Kingdom of Dalmatia.

III. THE DIVISIONS OF TRANSLEITHANIA. The lands of the Crown of St. Stephen were divided into counties (Comitats), which were administrative units. Historically Transleithania consisted of metropolitan Hungary (population 15,537,000) into which were incorporated Transylvania (2,678,000) and the port city of Fiume (50,000), and the Kingdom of Croatia-Slavonia (2,622,-000).

IV. NATIONALITIES IN CISLEITHANIA.

Germans		9,950,000
Slav speaking peoples:	Czechs	6,436,000
	Poles	4,968,000
	Ukrainians	3,519,000
Southern Slavs:	Slovenes	1,253,000
	Serbo-Croats	783,000
Latin speaking peoples:	Italians	768,000
	Rumanians	275,000

Lower Austria, Upper Austria, Salzburg, Vorarlberg, were purely German. In Styria and Carinthia the majority was German but there were strong Slovene minorities. Tyrol had a German majority with a very strong Italian minority. Carniola was practically Slovene.

In Bohemia and Moravia the Czechs formed the majority but there was a strong German minority. In

Silesia there was no majority. In order of numerical strength there were Germans, Poles, and Czechs.

In Galicia the Poles formed the majority but the Ukrainians represented a very strong minority. In Bukovina there was no majority. In numerical strength there lived Ukrainians, Rumanians, and Germans.

Along the Adriatic coast the Italians had the majority in Trieste and represented large minorities in Görz and Istria, where southern Slavs were the majority. Dalmatia was practically Serbo-Croatian in its population.

V. NATIONALITIES IN TRANSLEITHANIA.

Magyars		9,945,000
Germans		2,037,000
Rumanians		2,949,000
Slav speaking peoples:	Slovaks	1,968,000
	Croats	1,833,000
	Serbs	1,106,000
	Ukrainians	473,000

THE ABORTIVE COMPROMISE OF 1871 WITH THE CZECHS[1]

In 1871 the Hohenwart-Schäffle ministry tried to achieve a Compromise with the Czechs, similar to that achieved in 1867 with the Magyars. A. J. P. Taylor of Oxford University analyzes the negotiations and the reasons for their failure.

⌐   ⌐   ⌐

The practical expression of the Hohenwart-Schäffle policy was an attempt to arrive at a compromise with Bohemia, similar to the compromise reached with Hungary four years before; and the course of these negotiations illustrated once more the falsity of the analogy between the two countries. The Czech spokesmen, Rieger and Clam-Martinic, were not claiming, as the Magyars had been, the restoration of historic rights which had recently been lost; nor did they represent a nation which, within its own area, possessed a cultural and political monopoly. The Czechs demanded, not that imperial authority should be withdrawn from Bohemia, but that imperial authority should be used to give the Czechs political equality with the Germans. Yet at the very moment when the Czech leaders thus recognised that Czech freedom was to be created, not restored, they also put forward demands which implied that the lands of the Bohemian crown had never ceased to be a living

[1] A. J. P. Taylor, *The Habsburg Monarchy 1815-1918* (London: The Macmillan Co., Ltd., 1941), pp. 176-181. Reprinted by permission.

historic unit: they insisted that any national settlement must apply to Moravia and Silesia as well as to the province of Bohemia, and they proposed that, when Francis Joseph had been crowned King of Bohemia, the Imperial Council [*Reichsrat*] should be transformed from a central parliament (or pseudo-parliament) into a "Congress of Delegates" from the provinces, so that Austria would become a federal state. Their federalism was a further confession that Bohemia and Hungary were not the same; the Hungarians had insisted on Dualism to show that they, and they alone, were independent of Vienna, while the Czech support of federalism implied—which was indeed the case—that there was no living difference between Bohemia and the other provinces of the unitary Austrian state.

The Czech demands, or Fundamental Articles of 1871, were the culminating point of the mistaken attempt to win national autonomy by giving it a pseudo-historic disguise, and the falsity of the disguise brought the inevitable penalty of failure. The Hohenwart ministry proposed to solve the language question by making both German and Czech official tongues and allowing the communes, the units of local government, to use either; but the "subsidiary language" (i.e. either Czech or German) was also to be legal in Prague and in any commune where it was the language of one-fifth of the electors. This proposal favoured the Germans, who, being richer than the Czechs, benefited from the high property qualification and so could more often assure their one-fifth minority; moreover, the Germans were not one-fifth of the population of Prague. In the Bohemian Diet one-third of the members must be "Bohemian" (i.e. Czech) and one-quarter German, again a proportion more favourable to the Germans than their numbers warranted. The Czech negotiators raised no objection to thus treating the Germans with generosity; but they demanded the inclusion of Moravia and Silesia in the settlement, and the federal remodelling of Austria. By this false move they enabled the Germans of Bohemia to ride off from the details of the national compromise and to rally the Germans throughout the Empire, and

the Magyars as well, to the defence of their threatened
position. In Moravia, where the Czechs, though in a
majority, were less conscious than in Bohemia, the Diet
accepted the arrangement as regards the two languages,
but would agree only to equal representation of Czechs
and Germans in the Diet; in Silesia, where the original
Czech population had been reduced to a minority by
German encroachment, the Diet rejected the proposals
entirely. . . .

The Germans alone might not have turned Francis
Joseph from the policy of the Hohenwart ministry. The
German middle-class liberals were very much out of
favour, and their disapproval of the proposals tended
rather to recommend them to the Emperor; further,
Hohenwart and other aristocratic leaders were themselves
Germans—but from a class which Francis Joseph greatly
preferred to the lawyers and pedants of the bourgeois
ministry. The opposition of the Magyars was a different
matter. Andrássy had always realised that a settlement
in Bohemia would destroy Hungarian predominance in
the Empire and shake Magyar control even within Hungary. The Czechs, elevated to the rank of an imperial
nation, would be no longer indifferent to the condition
of the Hungarian Slavs; and their attack on Magyar
supremacy would be supported by those Germans who
remained loyal to the Empire, once German supremacy
had been destroyed elsewhere. On the other hand, those
Germans who could not accept equality with the Slav
peoples would advocate the destruction of the Habsburg
Empire, the inevitable result of which must be the sub-
ordination of Hungary to a Greater Germany—unless,
indeed, Russia came to the rescue of her Slav brethren,
which would be even worse.

To meet the danger of an Austria free from national
conflicts, Andrássy employed once more all the diplomatic talent which had brought the Hungarian cause to
victory four years earlier. Far from thrusting himself
forward with objections, he retired to a remote country
seat, confident that difficulties would arise which would
make Francis Joseph turn to him for advice; nor was he
mistaken. The first steps of the Hohenwart ministry

naturally produced protests from the Germans and riots among students in Vienna, the position of which as capital always acted as a magnifying-glass for German discontents; and Hohenwart and Schäffle, whose program had been elaborated in the quiet of the study, were at a loss how to proceed. Inevitably Francis Joseph turned to Andrássy, knowing that he would receive from him a confident, resolute answer; and Andrássy, after a show of reluctance, arrived in Vienna as an all-powerful arbitrator, the game already won. Andrássy did not conceal his contempt for the Bohemian program and declared that the proposed election of the Austrian Delegation by the provincial Diets was comparable to electing the Hungarian Delegation by the county meetings—a depreciation indeed of the "historic" provinces. He at once put his finger on the weak point of the Bohemian compromise when he said to Hohenwart: "Are you prepared to carry through the recognition of Bohemian state rights with cannon? If not, do not begin this policy"; and Hohenwart did not dare to answer him. The Bohemian demands had been meant as the beginning of a process of "bargaining," similar to Deák's program of 1861 which had only gradually evolved into the concessions of 1865. But the Czechs were given no opportunity of bargaining. Their refusal to be content with Hohenwart's first offer made Francis Joseph lose patience and so succumb to Andrássy's opposition. Negotiations were broken off, the Hohenwart ministry dismissed, and Francis Joseph returned to the bourgeois ministry of doctrinaire German liberals as the only alternative.

— Reading No. 13 —

THE DIFFICULT ART OF
GOVERNING AUSTRIA[1]

Perhaps the best description of the difficulties faced by Austria in the 1890's is provided by A. J. P. Taylor in his discussion of the consequences of a decision whether classes in the secondary school at Cilli in southern Styria should be conducted in German or in Slovene.

✓　　　　✓　　　　✓

Then came the coalition ministry, hastily collecting its majority by the widespread distribution of miscellaneous promises, and what more natural than to confirm the promise made to the Slovenes as far back as 1888? But, once the ministry began to execute its promises, the difficulty of the Cilli secondary school became overwhelming: if it was carried out, the Germans—not merely the German representatives from Styria, but the entire German block—would withdraw from the government; if it was not carried out, the Slovenes would withdraw and carry the Czechs, their fellow Slavs, with them. Cilli was the major political question of 1894, the Germans refusing to give way—or, as the phrase went, "to abandon the pioneers of German culture in the south"—and the government trying to persuade the Slovenes to be satisfied with a grammar school, exclusively Slovene, in some other town where the Germans had no traditional footing. No compromise could be reached, and finally,

[1] A. J. P. Taylor, *The Habsburg Monarchy 1815-1918* (London: Macmillan, 1941), pp. 213-217. Reprinted by permission.

in June 1895, the government carried through the Imperial Council a grant for Slovene classes in the Cilli grammar school; the Germans withdrew from the ministry, and the parliamentary coalition was broken up.

The story of Cilli amply illustrates all the disastrous weaknesses of the Austrian system. None of the political leaders had any conception of responsibility, except to their own parliamentary group; many of them admitted the need for a strong Empire, and few indeed had any ambition to destroy it, but they felt that "authority" would look after imperial needs. The Austrian ministers never recognised that they were the "authority"; to become a minister was merely to secure a stronger position for bargaining for particular interests. Moreover, the determination of what should have been local questions (though with a broad imperial line of principle) by the imperial government and the Imperial Council [Reichsrat] meant that these questions were decided not according to local strength, but according to the national balance throughout Austria. The Germans managed to hold up the Slovene classes at Cilli, not because they were strong at Cilli, nor even in Styria, but because German Bohemians, Germans from Vienna, and even Germans from the Bukovina, rallied to the defence of the national cause. And in the same way the Slovenes got their classes at Cilli, not because the Slovene population of Cilli increased, nor because they won a majority in the Styrian Diet, but because the Czechs and the Little Russian [Ukrainian] representatives from beyond the Carpathians could put pressure on the government. There can be here no question of assigning responsibility or of apportioning blame. The petty national struggles of the parliamentary groups seemed to justify the Emperor's retaining the real authority in his own hands; but it was because the political parties had no control over vital issues that they wasted their strength in these futile conflicts. Every year the evil became worse; the Emperor still more determined not to share his power with the irresponsible politicians, and the politicians ever more irresponsible because they had no share of power.

The preoccupation of the parties and of the Imperial

Council with local matters instead of with affairs of state gave, moreover, an entirely false picture of the feeling throughout Austria. It would be quite wrong to imagine that the vast majority burned with national grievances or were conscious either of oppression or injustice. The national politicians were a tiny minority, and the various organisations which deliberately tried to turn the national balance one way or the other never drew on much popular support. National grievances were felt only by the intellectuals who aspired to be school teachers, lawyers, university professors, or state officials; but it was this class which supplied the political spokesmen, and they voiced only the demands which they knew and themselves understood. The very extent of state activities— education, railways, the encouragement of industry by tariffs and subsidies—made Austria peculiarly vulnerable to national conflicts; she was now paying the penalty for never having had the sphere of state interference circumscribed during a successful period of *laissez-faire*. The incompetent manufacturer with his profits declining, the university student who failed to secure a degree, the lawyer who lost his case, all found an easy excuse in a central government allegedly hostile to their particular nationality, and it was only men with these and similar grievances who expressed themselves in politics. The ordinary citizen of the Empire was silent, as he had been silent for centuries; he was glad that "authority" was looking after affairs of state without a great burden of taxation, and he found "authority" friendly and sympathetic, though pedantic and slow like all bureaucracies, in his few dealings with it. But if ever the ordinary man wanted political excitement, he would seek it not in patriotic demonstrations for the Emperor, but in factitious grievances which were suddenly presented to him by a nationalistic spokesman. In these years ordinary men were discovering, to their great astonishment, that they had been nationally oppressed all their lives and that they must stand up for their rights. The simple German was told by reputable scholars that Austria had once been a German state, with German as the "language of state," and all the great cities of the Empire centres of

German culture; it was so no longer and he must organise in order to prevent the extermination of his people. The Czech peasant learnt from his schoolmaster that Bohemia had once been a Czech country, that the Germans were interlopers, and that they would once more disappear when the Czech people received fair play. If any of these peoples had lived in Hungary, they would have known what national oppression really meant; but unfortunately a sense of grievance is as violent and disruptive as the grievance itself.

In the thirty years after the making of Dualism, when national disputes had gradually been allowed to advance to the centre of the political stage, there had been little attempt to create any counter-feeling of loyalty to Austria or to bring to birth any new imperial idea. Conscious "Austrian" feeling existed among the nobility, and to an increasing extent the bureaucracy too forgot its old feud with the great landowners. But these two classes were debarred by their position and outlook from any contact with the peoples. The nobility, without any national roots, regarded the Austrian people as an extension of their own peasantry—their function to keep the nobility in luxury and, while deserving of paternal kindness, quite unfitted to play any active part in politics. The bureaucracy, for their part, knew the people only as the objects of administration; as well ask their desks to show an Austrian spirit as to expect an Austrian patriotism from the masses.

— Reading No. 14 —

MAGYARIZATION IN HUNGARY[1]

Of the difficulties which Slovaks and Rumanians suffered in Hungary in the last years before World War I Professor Arthur J. May of the University of Rochester gives the following description.

✦   ✦   ✦

While the intensification of the Magyarization process was directed against all minority groups, it was given special point by political stirrings among the Slovaks, the sequel to a modest cultural renaissance. Unhappily, the Slovak movement was gravely handicapped by Magyar educational policies which tended to convert educated Slovaks into Magyarones and by wide political differences among the handful of patriotic Slovak intellectuals. An older group preferred to write in the Slovak language, a regional variant of Czech, cherished strong Russophile sympathies, and in politics desired merely the autonomy of the Slovak counties within the Hungarian framework. But in the nineties a new literary faction emerged which acknowledged the community of interest and tradition with the Czechs, wrote in the Czech language, and advocated political unity with the Czechs. . . .

The attention of Europe was drawn to the Slovaks in 1907 by the notorious Csernova affair. Customarily

[1] Arthur J. May, *The Hapsburg Monarchy 1867-1914* (Cambridge, Mass.: Harvard University Press, 1951), pp. 378 f., 443 f. Reprinted by permission.

Magyarones [Magyarized Slovaks] were appointed to
Roman Catholic bishoprics in the Slovak area, but among
the lower clergy an occasional Slovak nationalist was
found. Such an one was Father Andreas Hlinka, for
forty years a sturdy apostle of Slovak rights and interests.
Born of simple Slovak peasant stock, Hlinka was or-
dained a priest in 1889 and quickly achieved local renown
as a fighter for the economic and cultural liberties of
his countrymen. He helped to organize a cooperative
society and bank and edited a newspaper, *Slovak*. Settled
as priest in the village of Csernova, he harangued his
parishioners against Magyar rule, discriminations against
the Slovak language, and related matters.

On charges of seditious agitation, Hlinka was arrested, convicted, and sentenced to jail, and the Mag-
yarone hierarchy suspended him from his priestly office.
His parishioners, however, secured the consent of the
bishop for the consecration of a newly built church,
though they failed to obtain permission for Hlinka to
participate in the ceremonies. Rather, another priest was
instructed to repair to Csernova for the dedication; on the
way he was warned by partisans of Hlinka that if he
set foot in the village he would place his life in jeopardy.
Discreetly he turned back and other clerics, escorted by
an armed guard, were sent to inform the inflamed
villagers that the rites of dedication had been postponed.
As the cavalcade approached Csernova a mob pelted it
with a barrage of stones, injuring a priest and several
gendarmes. When the crowd refused to disperse guards-
men opened fire, killing sixteen and wounding four times
as many. Almost half a hundred villagers were arrested
and, after a perfunctory trial, were severely punished;
Hlinka's sister, the alleged ringleader of the "insur-
rection," was sentenced to three years in prison.

The sanguinary Csernova affray not only quickened
the Slovak national consciousness but excited general
indignation among Habsburg Slavs and called forth sharp
denunciations of Magyars in the press of Europe. To
all critics the Hungarian government and its unapologetic
apologists retorted that the inhabitants of Csernova had
been peaceful and contented until fanatical Slovak agi-

tators egged them on to challenge established authority. . . .

That Magyar treatment of the Rumanian minority was largely responsible for the lukewarmness of the kingdom of Rumania toward the alliance with the Central Powers was fully appreciated by German and Austrian statesmen. Time and time again the men of Berlin implored Habsburg leaders to make concessions to the Rumanians; William II, for example, discussed the problem at full length with Francis Ferdinand and begged him to do something to mitigate the dangerous tension. Such counsel the heir presumptive really did not require, for he had long been sympathetic toward Rumanians on both sides of the Carpathians and he had not concealed his friendly disposition nor his detestation of the denationalizing tactics of the Magyars.

On the way to visit Rumania in 1909, the Archduke was lustily cheered by Transylvanian Rumanians who lined the railway track and in Bucharest he freely declared his disapprobation of Magyar oppression of Rumanians. Francis Ferdinand derived real pleasure from the fact that Magyar politicians were irritated over the visit. In conversation with the German emperor, the Archduke upbraided Tisza for neglecting to conciliate the Rumanians and begged William II to exert influence on the Magyar statesman; instructions in that vein were actually dispatched to the German ambassador in Vienna. . . .

For all his well-known antipathy toward Rumanians, Tisza is said to have admitted the justice of certain of these demands, yet he felt (or said he felt) that Magyar politicians could not be brought around to make concessions. The nub of the matter was that Magyar chauvinists, stubborn, arrogant, prejudiced, looked upon the Rumanians, as indeed upon other minority stocks, as an inferior breed of humanity, whom it was a tradition to despise and a duty to Magyarize. By refusing to exert his great personal prestige to persuade his fellows to satisfy Rumanian expectations, at least in part, Tisza muffed an opportunity for which he, his Hungary, and the Dual Monarchy would one day pay the penalty.

Trials of Rumanian journalists continued to be frequent and punishments heavy. And petty incidents constantly bobbed up to envenom the Magyar-Rumanian
feud. For example, in order to extend the area of Magyar
speech, the cabinet at Budapest secured papal sanction
for the transfer of several Uniat parishes to the jurisdiction of the Magyar bishop in Debreczen and for the use
of Magyar as the liturgical language in these churches.
The Rumanian population that was affected by this dubious deal protested vehemently, the life of the bishop
was threatened, and early in 1914 a bomb actually ex-
ploded in the episcopal office, killing the vicar and two
others and wrecking the building. Possibly this crime was
intended to be a signal for a general rising in Transylvania against the lordship of the Magyars. The culprits
escaped abroad, evidently to Rumania. A Uniat priest
and several of his parishioners were imprisoned for in-
veighing against the use of the Magyar tongue in religious
services.

— Reading No. 15 —

THE DEMOCRATIC AUSTRIAN
ELECTIONS OF 1906[1]

On May 14, 1906, for the first time elections were
held in Austria on the basis of a general, direct, and
democratic suffrage. The outstanding results were on the
one hand a bewildering number of parties and on the
other hand the success of the Social Democrats, ably led
by Dr. Viktor Adler (1852-1918). The following discus-
sion of the results of the election was written by an
Austrian for a British monthly journal.

✦   ✦   ✦

The result of the elections of May 14, which has, it
is true, been considerably modified by the supplementary
elections, was very startling. Overwhelming successes of
the socialist candidates were reported from all parts of
the country. If we turn first to Bohemia, the most important part of the western division of the monarchy
and at all times the cockpit of Austrian political warfare,
we find that the discomfiture of the Young Czech party
was the most important feature of the first pollings. . . .
There seems little doubt that on May 14 many electors
in Bohemia who were not socialists gave their votes to
the socialist candidates, moved by a general feeling of
discontent caused by the unjust treatment of Bohemia
in the electoral bill to which most of the Young Czechs
had given their assent. The [supplementary] elections of
May 23 in Bohemia, as in other parts of the empire,
witnessed the rally of the nonsocialist parties; as already

[1] *Fortnightly Review,* London, July 1907.

mentioned, a considerable number of the members of the formerly dominant Young Czech party now obtained seats, as well as some men belonging to the more ancient, more conservative party known as the Old Czechs. A few seats were also won by the Radical party, whose platform included the re-establishment—in a modified form—of the ancient Bohemian constitution.

The party, however, that achieved the greatest success of the elections of May 23 was that known as the "agrarians," and it is to this party that the largest number of the representatives of Bohemia in the new parliament of Vienna will belong. Land is overtaxed in Austria to an almost incredible degree, and the peasants have succeeded in returning a considerable number of members specially pledged to protect the interests of landowners. The fate of the German deputies of Bohemia was yet more disastrous; their places were almost everywhere taken by socialists. An interesting feature of the election was the complete discomfiture of the so-called "Pan-Germanic" party, most of whose representatives were returned by the Germans of Bohemia. These men had attempted to establish, in a manner they were never able clearly to define, a closer connection between Austria and Germany. They had rendered themselves ridiculous by their abject devotion to Germania, who somewhat contemptuously rejected the wooing of her uncouth lovers. . . .

The "sister lands" of Bohemia—that is, Moravia and Silesia, both countries which have a mainly Slavic population—voted in a manner not dissimilar from that of Bohemia. It should, however, be noted that in Moravia a considerable number of the clericals were elected,—a fact that may not inconsiderably influence the state of parties in the new parliament.

As regards the German parts of Austria, the elections of Vienna, the capital of the empire, of course attract the most attention. That city had formerly held liberal views, but gradually became clerical through the almost unlimited influence which Dr. Karl Lueger acquired over the Viennese. This somewhat second-rate Cleon began life as a Liberal, but soon became a Jew-baiter or Anti-

Semite. Through the indomitable energy of Lueger, his party, which afterward assumed the name of Christian Socialists,—though it is really conservative or rather clerical,—widely extended its influence of power. As one of its leaders stated at a recent public meeting, this party now has "adherents among all Germany from the Lake of Constance to the Bukowina!" At the Vienna elections the Christian Socialists were successful, but hardly to so great an extent as had been anticipated. The liberals indeed only secured three seats, but the Christian Socialists, to whom the absence of Dr. Lueger through illness was very harmful, found more dangerous antagonists in the members of the socialist party. That party has been very ably organized by Dr. Adler, a man of exceptional talent, and one of the many brilliant leaders whom, from the time of Lassalle downward, the Semitic race has given to the socialists. Besides winning many seats in Vienna, the socialists have also won seats in provincial towns of Lower Austria, while they have won a seat even at Innsbruck and have captured the entire parliamentary representation of Linz, the capital of Upper Austria, and of Trieste, the great seaport of the empire. The former German Liberal party has been long split up into various factions, and has at the election lost largely both to the clericals and to the socialists. . . .

The Slovenes, who inhabit parts of Styria, Carinthia, and Carniola, have mainly elected representatives, who, though favorable to the claims of the Slavic populations which they represent, will consider it their principal duty to further the clerical policy which finds favor among the agricultural populations of the districts which elected them. In Galicia, which sends about a hundred representatives to the parliament of Vienna, the elections have only just ended. As already mentioned, the new electoral law greatly favored the Polish majority of the population at the expense of the Ruthenian minority. The Poles were therefore, on the whole, successful, though a certain number of Ruthenians obtained seats in the new parliament. Two Zionists elected by the Galician Jews will be members of the new parliament of Vienna.

Hardly ever, perhaps, in the annals of parliamentary

government, have elections resulted in so complete a
surprise as did those just held in Austria. The recent
defeat of the socialists in Germany led even experienced
statesmen to believe that they would be far more unsuc-
cessful in Austria, which, rightly or wrongly, has always
been considered a very conservative country. The extreme
moderation hitherto displayed by the socialists largely
contributed to their victory. It is a proof of the universal
veneration with which all Austrians look on their sovereign, that not a single disloyal cry was heard during
the recent elections,—and the socialists formed no exception in this respect.

— Reading No. 16 —

THE ALLIANCE OF AUSTRIA-HUNGARY WITH GERMANY[1]

After his retirement from office Prince Otto von Bismarck wrote his memoirs, in which he explained and justified his policy. In the following excerpts he begins with the events of the late summer of 1879.

When Emperor William went to Alexandrovo (Sept. 3), I had already made arrangements at Gastein for a meeting with Count Andrássy, which took place on August 27-28. When I had explained the situation to him he drew therefrom the following conclusion: To a Russo-French alliance the natural counterpoise is an Austro-German alliance. I answered that he had formulated the question to discuss which I had suggested our meeting, and we came readily to a preliminary understanding for a merely defensive alliance against a Russian attack on one of the two sides; but my proposition to extend the alliance to other than Russian attacks, found no favour with the Count . . .

Before my departure from Gastein I addressed (Sept. 10) the following letter to the King of Bavaria:

"Your Majesty was so gracious on a former occasion as to express your most exalted satisfaction with the efforts which I directed to the object of securing for the German Empire peace and friendship with both her great neighbors, Austria and Russia alike. In the course of the

[1] Bismarck, *Reflections and Reminiscences* (Leipzig: Tauchnitz, 1899), Vol. III, pp. 180-184, 197-198, 201-202.

last three years this problem has increased in difficulty, as Russian policy has come to be entirely dominated by the partly warlike tendencies of Panslavism. . . . The leading minister, in so far as such a minister there is at present in Russia, is the War Minister, Milutin. At his demand the peace, in which Russia is threatened by no one, has yet been followed by the mighty preparations which . . . have raised . . . the footing of the army of the West, which is kept ready for active service, by about 400,000 men. These preparations can only be intended as a menace to Austria or Germany, and the military establishments in the kingdom of Poland correspond to such a design. The War Minister has also . . . unreservedly declared that Russia must prepare for a war 'with Europe.'

"If it is indubitable that Czar Alexander, without desiring the war with Turkey, nevertheless waged it under stress of Panslavist influence, in consequence of the greater and more dangerous impression which the agitation at the back of it now makes on the mind of the Czar, we may readily apprehend that it may also succeed in obtaining Czar Alexander's sanction for further warlike enterprises on the western frontier. . . .

"Austria regards the restless Russian policy with as much disquietude as we, and seems to be inclined, for an understanding with us for common defence against a possible Russian attack on either of the two Powers.

"If the German Empire were to come to such an understanding with Austria, an understanding which should have in view the cultivation of peace with Russia as sedulously as before, but should also provide for joint defence in the event of an attack by her upon either of the allied powers, I should see in it an essential security for the peace of Europe. Thus mutually assured, both empires might continue their efforts for the further consolidation of the Three Emperors' Alliance. The German Empire in alliance with Austria would not lack the support of England, and the peace of Europe, the common interest of both empires, would be guaranteed by 2,000,000 fighting men. In this alliance, purely defensive as it would be, there would be nothing to excite jealousy in any quarter: for in the German Confederation the same mutual guarantee subsisted with the sanction of international law for fifty years after 1815. If no such understanding is come to, Austria will not be to blame if, under the influence of Russian threats, and uncertain of the attitude of Germany, she finally seeks an *entente cordiale* with either France or Russia. In the latter case, Germany, by reason of her relation to France, would be in danger of entire isolation on the Continent. Supposing, however, that Austria were to effect an *entente cordiale* with France and England, as in 1854, Germany, unless prepared for isolation, would be forced to unite with Russia alone, and, as I fear, to follow in the mistaken and perilous course of Russian domestic and foreign policy.

"If Russia compels us to choose between her and Austria, I believe that the disposition which Austria would display towards us would be conservative and peaceable, while that of Russia would be uncertain." . . .

Peace between Germany and Russia may be imperilled by the systematic fomentation of ill-feeling, or by the ambition of Russian or German military men who desire war before they grow too old to distinguish themselves in any other way. The Russian press must needs be characterised by stupidity and disingenuousness in an unusual degree for it to believe and affirm that German policy was determined by aggressive tendencies in concluding the Austrian, and thereafter the Italian, defensive alliance. The disingenuousness was less of Russian than of Polish-French, the stupidity less of Polish-French than of Russian origin. In the field of Russian credulity and ignorance Polish-French finesse won a victory over that want of finesse in which, according to circumstances, consists now the strength, now the weakness of German policy. In most cases an open and honourable policy succeeds better than the subtlety of earlier ages, but it postulates, if it is to succeed, a degree of personl confidence which can more readily be lost than gained.

The future of Austria, regarded in herself, cannot be reckoned upon with that certainty which is demanded when the conclusion of durable and, so to speak, organic treaties is contemplated. The factors which must be taken into account in this shaping are as manifold as is the mixture of her populations, and to their corrosive and occasionally disruptive force must be added the incalculable influence that the religious element may from time to time, as the power of Rome waxes or wanes, exert upon the directing personalities. Not only Panslavism and the Bulgarian or Bosnian, but also the Serbian, the Roumanian, the Polish, the Czech questions, nay even today the Italian question in the district of Trent, in Trieste, and on the Dalmatian coast, may serve as points of crystallisation not merely for Austrian, but for European crises, by which German interests will be directly affected only in so far as the German Empire enters into a relation of close solidarity with Austria. In Bohemia the antagonism between Germans and Czechs has in some places penetrated so deeply into the army that the officers of the two nationalities in certain regiments hold aloof from one another even to the degree that they will not meet at mess. There is more immediate danger for Germany of becoming involved in grievous and dangerous struggles on her western frontier, by reason of the aggressive, plundering instincts of the French people, which have been greatly developed by her monarchs since the time of Emperor Charles V., in their lust of power at home as well as abroad . . .

We must and can honourably maintain the alliance with the Austro-Hungarian monarchy; it corresponds to our interests, to the historical traditions of Germany, to the public opinion of our people. The influences and forces under and amid which the future policy of Vienna must be shaped, are, however, more complex than with us, by reason of the manifold diversity of the nationalities, the divergence of their aspirations and activities, the influence of the clergy, and the temptation to which the Danubian countries are exposed in the Balkan and Black Sea latitudes.

We cannot abandon Austria, but neither can we lose sight of the possibility that the policy of Vienna may willy-nilly abandon us. The possibilities which in such a case remain open to us must be clearly realized and steadily borne in mind by German statesmen before the critical moment arrives, nor must their action be determined by prejudice or misunderstanding, but by an entirely dispassionate weighing of the national interests.

— Reading No. 17 —

AUSTRO-HUNGARIAN ADMINISTRATION OF BOSNIA [1]

The Austro-Hungarian administration found itself after 1878 in Bosnia-Herzegovina in the position of an advanced country administering an underdeveloped one. The problems faced there are similar to those faced in the twentieth century in Asia and Africa.

✓ ✓ ✓

Such colonial enterprise as the Danube Monarchy manifested was confined to Bosnia-Herzegovina. After 1878 when Austria occupied and undertook the administration of the region, economic and cultural affairs experienced a distinct, one might almost say a phenomenal improvement. Prosperity such as was not surpassed elsewhere in the Balkans, if indeed it was equaled, replaced the anarchy and devastation that had filled the long centuries of Turkish governance. Even a severe British critic of the Monarchy in general saw fit to write in 1908 that "the transformation wrought in Bosnia and Herzegovina by the Danube Monarchy, though naturally distasteful to Belgrade and Cetinje, has no modern parallel, save in the Egypt of Lord Cromer."

An official survey of Bosnia, carried out in 1906, revealed a great deal concerning the Hapsburg stewardship. Population had grown by more than half since Austria assumed charge—mute testimony in itself to the peace

[1] Arthur J. May, *The Hapsburg Monarchy 1867-1914* (Cambridge, Mass.: Harvard University Press, 1951), pp. 406-409. Reprinted by permission.

and order that prevailed. And whereas in 1878 there had been less than 600 miles of roads and only the faintest beginning of a railway system, by 1906 there were fully 4,000 miles of highways and 900 miles of railways, and the trackage would have been even greater had not Hungary raised objections to expansion. Native Bosnian spokesmen, it is true, contended that strategic interests of the Monarchy rather than commercial usefulness had largely determined the routes of transportation.

Bosnian industry, especially carpetmaking and the working of metals, had grown even in the face of stiff competition from machine-made wares in the Monarchy proper. With mixed success, the Bosnian government operated mines, and beginnings were made in the efficient exploitation of the forests that covered over half the province. Public revenues had risen prodigiously, partly because of more efficiency in the collection of taxes. Schooling facilities had been considerably extended; primary education was furnished by the government, which also subsidized schools conducted by religious bodies, but attendance was not compulsory. Specially talented Bosnian students were taken to Vienna on scholarships, which might, however, be revoked if the holders engaged in political activities; some students preferred Belgrade to Vienna, where they divided their time between study, idle vagabonding, and participation in the doings of Serbian political societies.

Under government auspices a few specialized agricultural schools, model farms, and breeding studs were established. In places excellent irrigation and water-supply systems were built, and the state furnished physicians and hospitals; medical and hygienic improvements indeed were noteworthy achievements of Austrian administration. Plain but comfortable hotels were built to attract tourists; Ilidže, an ancient watering place near Sarajevo, was converted into an attractive health resort and vacation spot.

The admirable Austrian gendarmerie, backed by a large military garrison, wrought something approaching a miracle in making life and property safe. Violence and rapine were less common than anywhere else in the

Balkans, and murders and manslaughter were even rarer than in Bavaria or East Prussia. The civil administration contained a large proportion of capable and conscientious officials; about a fourth of them were Bosnians, employed mostly, to be sure, in the lower ranks of the service. Religious creeds were treated impartially, which stirred resentment on all sides; the acutely competitive spirit of the rival sects was, however, somewhat mitigated by the compulsory tolerance enforced by the Austrian ruler. As of 1895, and ratios were little altered thereafter, about 43 per cent of the population professed the Orthodox faith, 34 per cent were Moslems, and 21 per cent Roman Catholic.

However impressive the material and social advancement which Hapsburg occupation brought, the fundamental problem of liberating the *kmets* (tenant peasants) from grasping landlords remained unsolved. The institution of primitive tenantry lay at the root of much of the discontent that existed in the provinces. For the greater part the cultivated land was worked by sharecroppers whose rights and duties were defined in a Turkish statute of 1859, which the Hapsburg administration preserved; as a rule, a tenth of the crops passed to the government, a third of the remainder to the landowner (*beg*), and the balance to the peasant cultivator. . . .

The Austrian administration hesitated to inaugurate radical innovations in the tenure of land, for the officials required the good will of the wealthy and they were concerned to prove to other Balkan Moslems that Austria could govern in an acceptable fashion. For the same reason, Moslem legal and religious customs were scrupulously respected and the faithful were even permitted to celebrate the Turkish sultan's birthday. While Benjamin Kállay was chief administrator, tenants were assisted in buying land. They could borrow up to half the purchase price from the government at 7 per cent; the rest they had to save or obtain privately at exorbitant rates. Count Stephen Burián, who succeeded Kállay in 1903, arranged with a Hungarian banking house to advance to the peasant all the money needed to purchase the land he worked. Loans would be repaid in installments, and the government assumed liability for what the peasant might fail to pay. That plan was replaced in 1911 by a government credit scheme whereby the tenant would become the owner of his holding by paying for it over a period of years. Landlords, however, were not obliged to dispose of their land, though compulsory sale was being seriously considered in official circles in 1914. Many peasants who took advantage of the government lending scheme soon found themselves hopelessly in arrears and on the outbreak of war in 1914 the whole project was abandoned. . . .

Failure of the Austrian administration to solve the land problem was only one of the deep grievances of the Orthodox (generally Serb) population of Bosnia. Intensely conservative, this element resented most of the social and political changes that had been introduced by the alien "Schwabs" [German-speaking officials]. They protested increases in taxation, prohibitions on the carrying of arms and of massacring Moslems, and forestry regulations, which restricted hunting, fishing, and the cutting of timber. And they complained bitterly against compulsory military service, exacted of all young men, and the sending of recruits outside of Bosnia for their training, as was generally done.

Orthodox Serb intellectuals, moreover, heatedly inveighed against limitations on civil freedoms, charged that their churches and schools were given less financial assistance than Roman Catholic institutions, and complained that commercial concessions and government contracts were granted only to Roman Catholics and to foreigners. There was yet another source of dissatisfaction among the politically articulate: the limited rights allowed natives in government. True, a consultative assembly composed of Bosnian high churchmen and a dozen laymen had been created to tender advice to the Austrian viceroy, and the larger towns had certain rights of home rule, but native politicians desired an elective legislature which would have authority over purely provincial affairs. Governor Burián acknowledged the validity of that claim and recommended in 1907 that a local assembly of some sort should be established.

THE ANNEXATION OF BOSNIA-HERZEGOVINA[1]

The official announcement of the annexation of the two former Turkish provinces came in a proclamation issued by the Austrian Emperor to the people of the two provinces.

✓   ✓   ✓

We, Francis Joseph, Emperor of Austria, King of Bohemia, and Apostolic King of Hungary, to the inhabitants of Bosnia and Herzegovina:

When a generation ago our troops crossed the borders of your lands, you were assured that they came not as foes, but as friends, with the firm determination to remedy the evils from which your fatherland had suffered so grievously for many years. This promise given at a serious moment has been honestly kept. It has been the constant endeavour of our government to guide the country by patient and systematic activity to a happier future.

To our great joy we can say that the seed then scattered in the furrows of a troubled soil has richly thrived. You yourselves must feel it a boon that order and security has replaced violence and oppression, that trade and traffic are constantly extending, that the elevating influence of education has been brought to bear in your country, and that under the shield of an orderly administration every man may enjoy the fruits of his labours.

It is the duty of us all to advance steadily along this path. With this goal before our eyes, we deem the mo-

[1] *London Weekly Times,* October 9, 1908.

ment come to give the inhabitants of the two lands a new proof of our trust in their political maturity. In order to raise Bosnia and Herzegovina to a higher level of political life we have resolved to grant both of those lands constitutional governments that are suited to the prevailing conditions and general interests, so as to create a legal basis for the representation of their wishes and needs. You shall henceforth have a voice when decisions are made concerning your domestic affairs, which, as hitherto, will have a separate administration. But the necessary premise for the introduction of this provincial constitution is the creation of a clear and unambiguous legal status for the two lands.

For this reason, and also remembering the ties that existed of yore between our glorious ancestors on the Hungarian throne and these lands, we extend our suzerainty over Bosnia and Herzegovina, and it is our will that the order of succession of our House be extended to these lands also. The inhabitants of the two lands thus share all the benefits which a lasting confirmation of the present relation can offer. The new order of things will be a guarantee that civilization and prosperity will find a sure footing in your home.

— Reading No. 19 —

THE OLD EMPEROR[1]

Joseph Redlich (1896-1936) was an Austrian student of English government and from 1907 to 1918 a member of the Austrian parliament. He knew Emperor Francis Joseph in the last decades of his life. With the Emperor playing a central role, the following description of his life after the suicide of the heir to the throne (1889) may be of interest.

✓   ✓   ✓

Silence reigned about the old Emperor in the Hofburg after the death of his son and the marriage of his youngest daughter. The Empress had resumed her old habit of travelling abroad and was but rarely and for short periods in Vienna; her health was again precarious, and she went regularly to the baths at Kissingen, Nauheim, and Wiesbaden, as well as doing all sorts of special cures. In the winter she again generally went to the Mediterranean countries, frequently visited various parts of northern Africa and Spain, and sometimes passed her time in the villa she had had built on the Island of Corfu, the Achilleon, though she began to care less for it than once had been the case. In art and literature she had long been specially attracted by Hellenism, both classical and modern. For many years, her small suite had included a Greek reader, a post latterly filled by M. Christomanos,

[1] Joseph Redlich, *Emperor Francis Joseph of Austria. A Biography* (New York: The Macmillan Company, 1929), pp. 472-476, 479-484. Reprinted by permission.

whose subsequent reminiscences have preserved many interesting sayings and characteristic traits of Elizabeth's.

For years now the relations between husband and wife had settled into friendship. Franz Joseph's view of woman was full of genuine chivalry and he had for Elizabeth a deep and reverent admiration; where her wishes were concerned, he was boundlessly generous. Thrifty as he was, and increasingly so, he did not mind what she spent on her journeys: nothing was too much for her. Every year, as a rule in the winter, he would himself travel to join her, usually in the south. Between them, a regular and constant interchange of letters and telegrams was kept up. For the Emperor this was a matter of the first importance.

This strong interest in each other's personal welfare was the basis of the relation between the imperial couple, both now well advanced in years. Elizabeth took no interest in politics, and the Emperor had no understanding of her hyper-intellectual life: though his attitude to it was always respectful, any share in it was for him impossible. Any hopes the Empress may ever have entertained of communion, here, had long been given up. Her life, in the years that remained to her after the Crown Prince's death, was often remote even from the small and carefully selected group that surrounded her, deep as was their devotion to her. Dark shadows lay across her way; she suffered incessant pain over the son's death, self-reproach, and, at times, physical agony. Only with her younger daughter was she on terms of intimate affection. In Vienna, no one missed her. In the cities of the monarchy she had become a complete stranger. In Switzerland, Italy, or elsewhere abroad she lived and travelled incognito under the title of the Countess Hohenembs.

In her correspondence with the Emperor she employed a singular name for him, the Greek word "Megaliotis," the "Great Lord." She well knew that he missed her more, year by year, than he had done in their earlier epochs; she knew that her constant absence deprived him of the one being with whom he could and would speak confidentially, and as one human being to another. Indeed, so far as the Emperor was concerned, anything like a private life and a purely human interchange of mind was possible only when he had the Empress with him. Friendship, as we know, he never had cultivated, and never could.

Shy and silent as he was, he, like any other man, had need of what we call "small talk": the relief and distraction given by the day-to-day conversations of intimates and the free interchange of opinions. Knowing this, the Empress sought to make good for the Emperor what he must lack altogether through her absence. Chance and the extraordinary tact of her woman's heart enabled her to do it.

Towards the end of the eighties, Franz Joseph had, at an audience, made the acquaintance of a court actress recently called to the imperial Burg Theatre—Frau Katharina Schratt. The charming and sympathetic appearance of this young woman—she was married to a certain Herr von Kiss and the mother of a son—immediately attracted the Emperor. She struck him at once as being, what she really was, the attractive embodiment of all that is best in the genuine Austrian woman, both in natural gayety, genuine simplicity, and a warmth of heart that was all her own. Grillparzer, in his finest dramas, presents such women, with all the creative insights of a great poet, as the fairest exponents of all that the culture of Old Austria meant both in the individual and in social life.

Born of good burgher parents in the old town of Baden near Vienna, an inner vocation took her to the stage. An artist of genuinely natural stamp, she was a great favorite with the public of Vienna and highly esteemed. If I am rightly informed, Empress Elizabeth knew her before the Emperor did, and was much attracted by her. There grew up in her mind an idea which developed into an eager desire to have this charming woman bring a little light and color into the Emperor's lonely, care-worn, and dreary life, darkened as it was by her own long and frequent absence. Soon, a visit to Frau Schratt became a precious habit with Franz Joseph, thanks in part to the charm of her conversation, which never touched on politics, and still more to her real tact, the tact which comes from the heart.

Elizabeth, in creating for Franz Joseph this friendship with Frau Schratt—she and her daughter both visited and received her regularly, especially at Ischl, near which she always spent the summer—once again gave him the best she had to give. How, otherwise, could Franz Joseph have endured his last quarter of a century of existence? Apart from his youngest daughter, who with her numerous children gave him something of the warmth of family life, he would not have had a single creature about him who treated him as a human being. Those about the Emperor learned to understand something of this when his worst though not his last tragedy overtook him. On September 10, 1898, the Italian anarchist, Luccheni, killed the noble Empress with a single stroke of his murderous weapon as she was in the act of stepping on board a steamer at Geneva. This frightful event smote Franz Joseph with all that his soul could still suffer in personal anguish. When, in a voice strangled with sobs, he said to one of his faithful generals, Count Paar, a man almost his own age, "The world does not know how much we loved each other," the words expressed not only bitter woe but an unspoken accusation of himself and fate.

From now on Franz Joseph was thrown back wholly on himself. . . .

Court life had been reduced to a minimum even before the Empress's death; after it, it remained so. The Emperor did not really take much notice of the Archdukes and was at no pains to establish contact even with the heirs to the throne. . . . The Emperor lived in the Hofburg. Since the middle of the nineties he had spent spring and autumn, and often later even the rigors of winter, in the charming old Palace of Schönbrunn. Even in his old age, he proceeded every day to the portion of the Hofburg he occupied to give audience and tirelessly receive the endless stream of ministers and diplomats, foreign ambassadors and envoys, and all the statesmen and officials whom he found it necessary to summon to deal with business.

His way of life and methods of work remained unaltered, in the form already described: both the general plan and all its details were meticulously regulated and conformed to. Now as then he strove to follow, to test, and to direct the working of the gigantic administrative machine of two great states and all that was comprised under their army—on the military and administrative sides and on that of technical progress, going as far as possible into details, especially in the case of the army. The task was vast and continually extending, but his love of detail and fondness for questions of personnel remained, with the result that, lost in details, he had often no power of fully grasping the real decisive points of fundamental problems involved. . . .

The picture that emerges from the recollections and observations of civil and military officers, who served in his household, can be summed up by saying: Francis Joseph in his age was the embodiment of the perfect gentleman on the throne of the last imperial German dynasty. This trait in him was unaffected by his harshest experiences and even the shrewdest blows dealt him by fate. The tragic case of General Benedek apart, hardly another instance can be cited in which he failed either in human understanding, or, in these latter days, in the gentleness of a nobleman ripened by much experience to any who served him or came in any way close to him.

Here is part of the explanation of the fact that every statesman and high official, every general and aide-de-camp,—all the people, in a word, who served as his assistants or advisors in his lofty task of sovereignty—fell under his spell, and stayed so, long after they had left his service. . . .

If, however, we turn to consider him as statesman, as constitutional monarch, we find the basic traits in his character only the more pronounced with the years—his dislike of being contradicted by or hearing anything disagreeable from his ministers leading, inevitably, to a progressive limitation of his awareness of the real condition of things in parliament and the government. Consultations between him and members of either house and privy councilors, whether they took place on the prime minister's initiative or spontaneously by these personages presenting themselves in audience, were apt to be fruitless, because the Emperor tended, in such case, only too generally, merely to take the standpoint of his prime minister. Thus everything depended on the character, insight, and gifts of this one man. When the prime minister was an aristocrat, . . . lacking the real political education, intellectual independence, and even, at times, the moral earnestness so great an office demands; or when he was a man disposed to seek safety in a Byzantine attitude and, as the phrase went, "spare" the Emperor from "worry"; or, instead of resigning, to talk about his unwillingness to leave the old Emperor in the lurch—then it would happen that great opportunities, such as could not be expected to recur, were missed, and errors committed which could only be retrieved with time and at a heavy cost to the authority of the government and of the crown.

Nor, with a monarchical government of this type, was it of much avail that the old Emperor was often far superior to his prime minister both in political experience and knowledge of men and things. What the recurrent crises really called for was the quality of moral force in the brain responsible for decision, and the power to use given facts and conditions in a constructive fashion. And here age had not given the Emperor capacity denied him in his youth.

— Reading No. 20 —

THE AUSTRIAN ULTIMATUM TO SERBIA IN 1914

On July 23, 1914, the Austro-Hungarian government presented to the Serbian government a note containing ten demands and summing up the complaints of the Austro-Hungarian monarchy regarding the subversive activities of Serbians directed against the monarchy, which, it was found, reached a climax in the assassination of the Austrian heir to the throne in Sarajevo, the capital of Bosnia, on June 28, 1914.

✦   ✦   ✦

On the 31st of March, 1909, the Serbian Minister in Vienna, on the instructions of the Serbian Government, made the following declaration to the Imperial and Royal Government:

"Serbia recognizes that the fait accompli regarding Bosnia has not affected her rights, and consequently she will conform to the decisions that the Powers may take in conformity with Article 25 of the Treaty of Berlin. In deference to the advice of the Great Powers, Serbia undertakes to renounce from now onwards the attitude of protest and opposition which she has adopted with regard to the annexation since last autumn. She undertakes, moreover, to modify the direction of her policy with regard to Austria-Hungary and to live in future on good neighborly terms with the latter."

The history of recent years, and in particular the painful events of the 28th June last, have shown the existence of a subversive movement with the object of detaching a part of the territories of Austria-Hungary from the

177

Monarchy. The movement which had its birth under the eye of the Serbian Government has gone so far as to make itself manifest on both sides of the Serbian frontier in the shape of acts of terrorism and a series of outrages and murders.

Far from carrying out the formal undertakings contained in the declaration of the 31th March, 1909, the Royal Serbian Government has done nothing to repress these movements. It has permitted the criminal machinations of various societies and associations directed against the Monarchy, and has tolerated unrestrained language on the part of the press, the glorification of the perpetrators of outrages, and the participation of officers and functionaries in subversive agitation. It has permitted an unwholesome propaganda in public instruction, in short, it has permitted all manifestations of a nature to incite the Serbian population to hatred of the Monarchy and contempt of its institutions.

This culpable tolerance of the Royal Serbian Government had not ceased at the moment when the events of the 28th June last proved its fatal consequences to the whole world.

It results from the depositions and confessions of the criminal perpetrators of the outrage of the 28th June that the Sarajevo assassinations were planned in Belgrade; that the arms and explosives with which the murderers were provided had been given to them by Serbian officers and functionaries belonging to the Narodna Odbrana; and finally that the passage into Bosnia of the criminals and their arms was organized and effected by the chiefs of the Serbian frontier service.

The above-mentioned results of the magisterial investigation do not permit the Austro-Hungarian Government to pursue any longer the attitude of expectant forbearance which they have maintained for years in the face of the machinations hatched in Belgrade, and thence propagated in the territories of the Monarchy. The results, on the contrary, impose on them the duty of putting an end to the intrigues which form a perpetual menace to the tranquillity of the Monarchy.

To achieve this end the Imperial and Royal Govern-

ment see themselves compelled to demand from the Royal
Serbian Government a formal assurance that they condemn this dangerous propaganda against the Monarchy;
in other words, the whole series of tendencies, the ulti-
mate aim of which is to detach from the Monarchy territories belonging to it; and that they undertake to suppress by every means this criminal and terrorist propaganda.

In order to give a formal character to this undertaking
the Royal Serbian Government shall publish on the front
page of their Official Journal of the 13/26 July the following declaration:

"The Royal Government of Serbia condemn the propaganda directed against Austria-Hungary—i.e. the general
tendency of which the final aim is to detach from the
Austro-Hungarian Monarchy territories belonging to it,
and they sincerely deplore the fatal consequences of
these criminal proceedings.

"The Royal Government regret that Serbian officers
and functionaries participated in the above-mentioned
propaganda and thus compromised the good neighborly
relations to which the Royal Government were solemnly
pledged by their declaration of March 31, 1909.

"The Royal Government, who disapprove and repu-
diate all idea of interfering or attempting to interfere
with the destinies of the inhabitants of any part whatsoever of Austria-Hungary, consider it their duty for-
mally to warn officers and functionaries and the whole
population of the kingdom, that henceforward they will
proceed with the utmost rigor against persons who may
be guilty of such machinations, which they will use all
their efforts to anticipate and suppress."

This declaration shall simultaneously be communi-
cated to the Royal Army as an order of the day by His
Majesty the King and shall be published in the Official
Bulletin of the Army.

The Royal Serbian Government further undertake:

1. To suppress any publication which incites to hatred
and contempt of the Austro-Hungarian Monarchy and
the general tendency of which is directed against its
territorial integrity;

2. To dissolve immediately the society styled "Narodna Odbrana," to confiscate all its means of propaganda, and to proceed in the same manner against other societies and their branches in Serbia which engage in propaganda against the Austro-Hungarian Monarchy. The Royal Government shall take the necessary measures to prevent the societies dissolved from continuing their activities under another name and form;

3. To eliminate without delay from public instruction in Serbia, both as regards the teaching body and also as regards the methods of instruction, everything that serves, or might serve, to foment the propaganda against Austria-Hungary;

4. To remove from the military service, and from the administration in general, all officers and functionaries guilty of propaganda against the Austro-Hungarian Monarchy whose names and deeds the Austro-Hungarian Government reserve to themselves the right of communicating to the Royal Government;

5. To accept the collaboration in Serbia of representatives of the Austro-Hungarian Government for the suppression of the subversive movement directed against the territorial integrity of the Monarchy;

6. To take judicial proceedings against accessories to the plot of the 28th June who are on Serbian territory; delegates of the Austro-Hungarian Government will take part in the investigation relating thereto;

7. To proceed without delay to the arrest of Major Voija Tankositch and of the individual named Milan Ciganovitch, a Serbian State employee, who have been compromised by the results of the magisterial inquiry at Sarajevo;

8. To prevent by effective measures the cooperation of the Serbian authorities in the illicit traffic in arms and explosives across the frontier, to dismiss and punish severely the officials of the frontier service in Schabatz and Loznica guilty of having assisted the perpetrators of the Sarajevo crime by facilitating their passage across the frontier;

9. To furnish the Imperial and Royal Government with explanations regarding the unjustifiable utterances

of high Serbian officials, both in Serbia and abroad, who, notwithstanding their official position, have not hesitated since the crime of 28th June to express themselves in interviews in terms of hostility to the Austro-Hungarian Government; and finally,

10. To notify the Imperial and Royal Government without delay of the execution of the measures comprised under the preceding heads.

The Austro-Hungarian Government expect the reply of the Royal Government by 6 o'clock on Saturday evening the 25th July.

A SHORT BIBLIOGRAPHY

Blum, Jerome, *Noble Landowners and Agriculture in Austria, 1815-1848*, Baltimore, Md.: Johns Hopkins University Press, 1948.

Halecki, Oscar, *A History of Poland*, New York: Roy Publishers, 1943.

Hallberg, Charles W., *Franz Joseph and Napoleon III, 1852-1864*, New York: Bookman Associates, 1955.

Jászi, Oscar, *The Dissolution of the Habsburg Monarchy*, Chicago: University of Chicago Press, 1929.

Jelavich, Charles and Barbara, *The Habsburg Monarchy: Toward a Multinational Empire or National States*, New York: Rinehart & Company, Inc., 1959.

Jenks, William A., *The Austrian Electoral Reform of 1907*, New York: Columbia University Press, 1950.

Kann, Robert A., *The Multinational Empire: Nationalism and National Reform in the Habsburg Monarchy, 1848-1918*, 2 vols., New York: Columbia University Press, 1950.

Kann, Robert A., *The Habsburg Monarchy, A Study in Integration and Disintegration*, New York: Praeger, 1957.

Kohn, Hans, *Pan-Slavism, History and Ideology*, new edition, New York: Vintage Books, 1960.

Kosáry, Dominic G., *A History of Hungary*, Cleveland: The Benjamin Franklin Bibliophile Society, 1941.

Langsam, Walter C., *Francis the Good: The Education of an Emperor, 1768-1792*, New York: Macmillan, 1949.

Lengyel, Emil, *1000 Years of Hungary*, New York: John Day, 1958.

Mamatey, Victor S., *The United States and East Central Europe, 1914-1918: A Study in Wilsonian Diplomacy and Propaganda*, Princeton, N.J.: Princeton University Press, 1957.

May, Arthur J., *The Hapsburg Monarchy, 1867-1914*, Cambridge, Mass.: Harvard University Press, 1951.

184   THE HABSBURG EMPIRE, 1804-1918

Meyer, Henry Cord, *Mitteleuropa in German Thought and Action, 1815-1945,* The Hague: Nijhoff, 1955.

Rath, R. John, *The Viennese Revolution of 1848,* Austin, Texas: University of Texas Press, 1957.

Redlich, Joseph, *Emperor Francis Joseph of Austria,* New York: Macmillan, 1929.

Schmitt, Bernadotte E., *The Annexation of Bosnia—1908-1909,* Cambridge: The University Press, 1937.

Sweet, Paul R., *Friedrich von Gentz, Defender of the Old Order,* Madison, Wis.: University of Wisconsin Press, 1941.

Seton-Watson, Robert William, *Racial Problems in Hungary,* London: Constable, 1908.

Seton-Watson, Robert William, *A History of the Roumanians,* Cambridge: The University Press, 1934.

Taylor, A. J. B., *The Habsburg Monarchy, 1815-1918,* London: Macmillan, 1941.

Thomson, S. Harrison, *Czechoslovakia in European History,* new edition, Princeton, N.J.: Princeton University Press, 1943.

Viereck, Peter, *Conservatism Revisited,* New York: Scribner, 1949.

INDEX

185

VAN NOSTRAND ANVIL BOOKS already published